Ninja Foodi Digital Air Fry Oven Cookbook 2021

1000-Days Easier & Crispier Recipes for Your Family and Friends

Yvette Shepard

TABLE OF CONTENTS

Introduction

The Ninja Foodi™ has launched the Ninja Foodi Digital Air Fry Oven a few months back, and reviews on the device are very promising. It comprises various cooking functions, including air frying, air broiling, baking, toasting, dehydrating, and keeping your food warm. All these features are available in a relatively smaller device giving you ample kitchen space and all the functions you can long for. In the initial days, the Ninja Foodi Digital Air Fry Oven was only available on the official online store of Ninja Foodi™, but recently it is put up for sale on prominent marketplaces like Walmart and Amazon.

Main functions of the Ninja Foodi Digital Air Fry Oven

The primary function of the Ninja Foodi Digital Air Fry Oven is air frying. Additionally, it can also perform various other cooking functions. These cooking functions make the Ninja Foodi Digital Air Fry Oven a compact device that serves almost every cooking function you might ever encounter in your kitchen. The specs of the cooking functions of the Ninja Foodi Digital Air Fry Oven are as follows:

1. It can **air fry** 4 pounds food in a single go with even crispiness and thorough frying. The taste of the food is better than regular fried food.

2. It can **toast** nine slices of bread at a time. It thoroughly toasts your bread evenly with perfect texture and brownness. It also offers high and medium toasting settings.
3. It is the best **air roaster** amongst all the air roasters manufactured by the Ninja Foodi™. You can make a perfect sheet pan dinner having four servings. 3 pounds of ingredients will take 22 minutes to air roast.
4. It can **bake** cakes and muffins by using a shallow pan. You can also bake cookies in your Ninja Foodi Digital Air Fry Oven. But an entire pan or a Bundt pan cannot fit in it.
5. You can quickly **air broil** a chicken breast merely in 30 minutes in the Ninja Foodi Digital Air Fry Oven. It will give your steak the perfect crisp and texture. However, you cannot fit a complete chicken in it.
6. It can quickly **dehydrate** your food while being noiseless. The average time taken by this device to perfectly dehydrate your food is approximately 10 to 11 hours.
7. You can **keep your food warm** on food-safe temperature ranges in the Ninja Foodi Digital Air Fry Oven for a relatively long time. It spares your reheating your food.

Benefits and Shortcomings of the Ninja Foodi Digital Air Fry Oven

The Ninja Foodi Digital Air Fry Oven offers a wide array of advantages. However, it also has a few shortcomings, which can be overshadowed by the feature it offers to the users. Some of the advantages of the Ninja Foodi Digital Air Fry Oven are stated below:

- Stainless steel body
- Digital control panel with easily understandable controls.
- Flip it on one side for saving space after using it.
- Small in size, noiseless, and energy saving.

Some notable disadvantages of the Ninja Foodi Digital Air Fry Oven are stated below:

- Due to its smaller size, it is impossible to fit an entire chicken in it.
- The price is relatively higher than traditional ovens. But, the higher price offers more functions.

Breakfast Recipes

Savory French Toast

Preparation Time: 10 minutes
Cooking Time: 5 minutes
Servings: 2
Ingredients:

- ¼ cup chickpea flour
- 3 tablespoons onion, finely chopped
- 2 teaspoons green chili, seeded and finely chopped
- ½ teaspoon red chili powder
- ¼ teaspoon ground turmeric
- ¼ teaspoon ground cumin
- Salt, to taste
- Water, as needed
- 4 bread slices

Preparation:

1. Add all the ingredients except bread slices in a large bowl and mix until a thick mixture form.
2. With a spoon, spread the mixture over both sides of each bread slice.
3. Arrange the bread slices into the lightly greased sheet pan.
4. Press "Power Button" of Ninja Foodi Digital Air Fry Oven and turn the dial to select "Air Fry" mode.
5. Press "Time Button" and again turn the dial to set the cooking time to 5 minutes.
6. Now push "Temp Button" and rotate the dial to set the temperature at 390 degrees F.
7. Press "Start/Pause" button to start.
8. When the unit beeps to show that it is preheated, open the lid and insert the sheet pan in oven.
9. Flip the bread slices once halfway through.
10. When cooking time is completed, open the lid and serve warm.

Serving Suggestions: Serve with the topping of butter.
Variation Tip: you can add herbs of your choice in flour batter.
Nutritional Information per Serving:
Calories: 151 | **Fat:** 2.3g|**Sat Fat:** 0.3g|**Carbohydrates:** 26.7g|**Fiber:** 5.4g|**Sugar:** 4.3g|**Protein:** 6.5g

Ricotta Toasts with Salmon

Preparation Time: 10 minutes
Cooking Time: 4 minutes
Servings: 2

Ingredients:

- 4 bread slices
- 1 garlic clove, minced
- 8 ounces ricotta cheese
- 1 teaspoon lemon zest
- Freshly ground black pepper, to taste
- 4 ounces smoked salmon

Preparation:

1. In a food processor, add the garlic, ricotta, lemon zest and black pepper and pulse until smooth.
2. Spread ricotta mixture over each bread slices evenly.
3. Press "Power Button" of Ninja Foodi Digital Air Fry Oven and turn the dial to select "Air Fry" mode.
4. Press "Time Button" and again turn the dial to set the cooking time to 4 minutes.
5. Now push "Temp Button" and rotate the dial to set the temperature at 355 degrees F.
6. Press "Start/Pause" button to start.
7. When the unit beeps to show that it is preheated, open the lid and insert the sheet pan in oven.
8. When cooking time is completed, open the lid and transfer the slices onto serving plates.
9. Top with salmon and serve.

Serving Suggestions: Serve with the garnishing of fresh herbs.

Variation Tip: Ricotta cheese can be replaced with feta.

Nutritional Information per Serving:

Calories: 274 | **Fat:** 12g|**Sat Fat:** 6.3g|**Carbohydrates:** 15.7g|**Fiber:** 0.5g|**Sugar:** 1.2g|**Protein:** 24.8g

Zucchini Fritters

Preparation Time: 15 minutes
Cooking Time: 7 minutes
Servings: 4

Ingredients:

- 10½ ounces zucchini, grated and squeezed
- 7 ounces Halloumi cheese
- ¼ cup all-purpose flour
- 2 eggs
- 1 teaspoon fresh dill, minced
- Salt and ground black pepper, as required

Preparation:

1. In a large bowl and mix together all the ingredients.
2. Make small-sized fritters from the mixture.
3. Press "Power Button" of Ninja Foodi Digital Air Fry Oven and turn the dial to select "Air Fry" mode.
4. Press "Time Button" and again turn the dial to set the cooking time to 7 minutes.
5. Now push "Temp Button" and rotate the dial to set the temperature at 355 degrees F.
6. Press "Start/Pause" button to start.
7. When the unit beeps to show that it is preheated, open the lid.
8. Arrange fritters into the greased sheet pan and insert in the oven.
9. When cooking time is completed, open the lid and serve warm.

Serving Suggestions: Serve with the topping of sour cream.

Variation Tip: Make sure to squeeze the zucchini completely.

Nutritional Information per Serving:

Calories: 253 | **Fat:** 17.2g|**Sat Fat:** 1.4g|**Carbohydrates:** 10g|**Fiber:** 1.1g|**Sugar:** 2.7g|**Protein:** 15.2g

Sweet Potato Rosti

Preparation Time: 15 minutes
Cooking Time: 15 minutes
Servings: 2

Ingredients:

- ½ pound sweet potatoes, peeled, grated and squeezed
- 1 tablespoon fresh parsley, chopped finely
- Salt and ground black pepper, as required

Preparation:

1. In a large bowl, mix together the grated sweet potato, parsley, salt, and black pepper.
2. Arrange the sweet potato mixture into the lightly greased sheet pan and shape it into an even circle.
3. Press "Power Button" of Ninja Foodi Digital Air Fry Oven and turn the dial to select "Air Fry" mode.
4. Press "Time Button" and again turn the dial to set the cooking time to 15 minutes.
5. Now push "Temp Button" and rotate the dial to set the temperature at 355 degrees F.
6. Press "Start/Pause" button to start.
7. When the unit beeps to show that it is preheated, open the lid and insert the sheet pan in oven.
8. When cooking time is completed, open the lid
9. Cut the potato rosti into wedges and serve immediately.

Serving Suggestions: Serve alongside the yogurt dip.

Variation Tip: Potato can also be used instead of sweet potato.

Nutritional Information per Serving:

Calories: 160 | **Fat:** 2.1g|**Sat Fat:** 1.4g|**Carbohydrates:** 30.3g|**Fiber:** 4.7g|**Sugar:** 0.6g|**Protein:** 2.2g

Cheddar & Cream Omelet

Preparation Time: 10 minutes
Cooking Time: 8 minutes
Servings: 2

Ingredients:

- 4 eggs
- ¼ cup cream
- 1 teaspoon fresh parsley, minced
- Salt and ground black pepper, as required
- ¼ cup Cheddar cheese, grated

Preparation:

1. In a bowl, add the eggs, cream, parsley, salt, and black pepper and beat well.
2. Place the egg mixture into a small baking pan.
3. Press "Power Button" of Ninja Foodi Digital Air Fry Oven and turn the dial to select "Air Fry" mode.
4. Press "Time Button" and again turn the dial to set the cooking time to 8 minutes.
5. Now push "Temp Button" and rotate the dial to set the temperature at 350 degrees F.
6. Press "Start/Pause" button to start.
7. When the unit beeps to show that it is preheated, open the lid.
8. Arrange pan over the wire rack and insert in the oven.
9. After 4 minutes, sprinkle the omelet with cheese evenly.
10. When cooking time is completed, open the lid and remove the baking pan.
11. Cut the omelet into 2 portions and serve hot.

Serving Suggestions: Serve alongside the toasted bread slices.

Variation Tip: You can add the seasoning of your choice.

Nutritional Information per Serving:

Calories: 202 | **Fat:** 15.1g|**Sat Fat:** 6.8g|**Carbohydrates:** 1.8g|**Fiber:** 0g|**Sugar:** 1.4g|**Protein:** 14.8g

Eggs, Tofu & Mushroom Omelet

Preparation Time: 15 minutes
Cooking Time: 35 minutes
Servings: 2

Ingredients:

- 2 teaspoons canola oil
- ¼ of onion, chopped
- 1 garlic clove, minced
- 3½ ounces fresh mushrooms, sliced
- 8 ounces silken tofu, pressed, drained and crumbled
- Salt and ground black pepper, as needed
- 3 eggs, beaten

Preparation:

1. In a skillet, heat the oil over medium heat and sauté the onion, and garlic for about 4-5 minutes.
2. Add the mushrooms and cook for about 4-5 minutes.
3. Remove from the heat and stir in the tofu, salt and black pepper.
4. Place the tofu mixture into a baking pan and top with the beaten eggs.
5. Press "Power Button" of Ninja Foodi Digital Air Fry Oven and turn the dial to select "Air Fry" mode.
6. Press "Time Button" and again turn the dial to set the cooking time to 25 minutes.
7. Now push "Temp Button" and rotate the dial to set the temperature at 355 degrees F.
8. Press "Start/Pause" button to start.
9. When the unit beeps to show that it is preheated, open the lid.
10. Arrange pan over the wire rack and insert in the oven.
11. When cooking time is completed, open the lid and remove the baking pan.
12. Cut into equal-sized wedges and serve hot.

Serving Suggestions: Serve alongside the greens.

Variation Tip: Make sure to drain the tofu completely.

Nutritional Information per Serving:

Calories: 224 | **Fat:** 14.5g|**Sat Fat:** 2.9g|**Carbohydrates:** 6.6g|**Fiber:** 0.9g|**Sugar:** 3.4g|**Protein:** 17.9g

Pancetta & Spinach Frittata

Preparation Time: 15 minutes
Cooking Time: 16 minutes
Servings: 2

Ingredients:

- ¼ cup pancetta
- ½ of tomato, cubed
- ¼ cup fresh baby spinach
- 3 eggs
- Salt and ground black pepper, as required
- ¼ cup Parmesan cheese, grated

Preparation:

1. Heat a nonstick skillet over medium heat and cook the pancetta for about 5 minutes.
2. Add the tomato and spinach cook for about 2-3 minutes.
3. Remove from the heat and drain the grease from skillet.
4. Set aside to cool slightly.
5. Meanwhile, in a small bowl, add the eggs, salt and black pepper and beat well.
6. In the bottom of a greased baking pan, place the pancetta mixture and top with the eggs, followed by the cheese.
7. Press "Power Button" of Ninja Foodi Digital Air Fry Oven and turn the dial to select "Air Fry" mode.
8. Press "Time Button" and again turn the dial to set the cooking time to 8 minutes.
9. Now push "Temp Button" and rotate the dial to set the temperature at 355 degrees F.
10. Press "Start/Pause" button to start.
11. When the unit beeps to show that it is preheated, open the lid.
12. Arrange pan over the wire rack and insert in the oven.
13. When cooking time is completed, open the lid and remove the baking dish.
14. Cut into equal-sized wedges and serve.

Serving Suggestions: Serve alongside the green salad.

Variation Tip: You can use bacon instead of pancetta

Nutritional Information per Serving:

Calories: 287 | **Fat:** 20.8g|**Sat Fat:** 7.2g|**Carbohydrates:** 1.7g|**Fiber:** 0.3g|**Sugar:** 0.9g|**Protein:** 23.1g

Ham & Egg Cups

Preparation Time: 10 minutes
Cooking Time: 18 minutes
Servings: 6

Ingredients:

- 6 ham slices
- 6 eggs
- 6 tablespoons cream
- 3 tablespoon mozzarella cheese, shredded
- ¼ teaspoon dried basil, crushed

Preparation:

1. Lightly grease 6 cups of a silicone muffin tin.
2. Line each prepared muffin cup with 1 ham slice.
3. Crack 1 egg into each muffin cup and top with cream.
4. Sprinkle with cheese and basil.
5. Press "Power Button" of Ninja Foodi Digital Air Fry Oven and turn the dial to select "Air Fry" mode.
6. Press "Time Button" and again turn the dial to set the cooking time to 18 minutes.
7. Now push "Temp Button" and rotate the dial to set the temperature at 350 degrees F.
8. Press "Start/Pause" button to start.
9. When the unit beeps to show that it is preheated, open the lid.
10. Arrange the muffin tin over the wire rack and insert in the oven.
11. When cooking time is completed, open the lid and place the muffin tin onto a wire rack to cool for about 5 minutes.
12. Carefully invert the muffins onto the platter and serve warm.

Serving Suggestions: Serve alongside the buttered bread slices.

Variation Tip: Use room temperature eggs.

Nutritional Information per Serving:

Calories: 156 | **Fat:** 10g|**Sat Fat:** 4.1g|**Carbohydrates:** 2.3g|**Fiber:** 0.4g|**Sugar:** 0.6g|**Protein:** 14.3g

Banana & Walnut Bread

Preparation Time: 15 minutes
Cooking Time: 25 minutes
Servings: 10
Ingredients:

- 1½ cups self-rising flour
- ¼ teaspoon bicarbonate of soda
- 5 tablespoons plus 1 teaspoon butter
- 2/3 cup plus ½ tablespoon caster sugar
- 2 medium eggs
- 3½ ounces walnuts, chopped
- 2 cups bananas, peeled and mashed

Preparation:

1. In a bowl, mix together the flour and bicarbonate of soda.
2. In another bowl, add the butter and sugar and beat until pale and fluffy.
3. Add the eggs, one at a time, along with a little flour and mix well.
4. Stir in the remaining flour and walnuts.
5. Add the bananas and mix until well combined.
6. Grease a loaf pan.
7. Place the mixture into the prepared pan.
8. Press "Power Button" of Ninja Foodi Digital Air Fry Oven and turn the dial to select the "Air Crisp" mode.
9. Press "Time Button" and again turn the dial to set the cooking time to 10 minutes.
10. Now push "Temp Button" and rotate the dial to set the temperature at 355 degrees F.
11. Press "Start/Pause" button to start.
12. When the unit beeps to show that it is preheated, open the lid.
13. Arrange the pan into the air fry basket and insert in the oven.
14. After 10 minutes of cooking, set the temperature at 338 degrees F for 15 minutes.
15. When cooking time is completed, open the lid and place the pan onto a wire rack to cool for about 10 minutes.
16. Carefully invert the bread onto the wire rack to cool completely before slicing.
17. Cut the bread into desired sized slices and serve.

Serving Suggestions: Serve with strawberry jam.
Variation Tip: Walnuts can be replaced with pecans.
Nutritional Information per Serving:
Calories: 270 | **Fat:** 12.8g|**Sat Fat:** 4.3g|**Carbohydrates:** 35.5g|**Fiber:** 2g|**Sugar:** 17.2g|**Protein:** 5.8g

Carrot & Raisin Bread

Preparation Time: 15 minutes
Cooking Time: 35 minutes
Servings: 8

Ingredients:

- 2 cups all-purpose flour
- 1½ teaspoons ground cinnamon
- 2 teaspoons baking soda
- ½ teaspoon salt
- 3 eggs
- ½ cup sunflower oil
- ½ cup applesauce
- ¼ cup honey
- ¼ cup plain yogurt
- 2 teaspoons vanilla essence
- 2½ cups carrots, peeled and shredded
- ½ cup raisins
- ½ cup walnuts

Preparation:

1. Line the bottom of a greased baking pan with parchment paper.
2. In a medium bowl, sift together the flour, baking soda, cinnamon and salt.
3. In a large bowl, add the eggs, oil, applesauce, honey and yogurt and with a hand-held mixer, mix on medium speed until well combined.
4. Add the eggs, one at a time and whisk well.
5. Add the vanilla and mix well.
6. Add the flour mixture and mix until just combined.
7. Fold in the carrots, raisins and walnuts.
8. Place the mixture into a lightly greased baking pan.
9. With a piece of foil, cover the pan loosely.
10. Press "Power Button" of Ninja Foodi Digital Air Fry Oven and turn the dial to select the "Air Crisp" mode.
11. Press "Time Button" and again turn the dial to set the cooking time to 30 minutes.
12. Now push "Temp Button" and rotate the dial to set the temperature at 347 degrees F.
13. Press "Start/Pause" button to start.
14. When the unit beeps to show that it is preheated, open the lid.
15. Arrange the pan into the air fry basket and insert in the oven.
16. After 25 minutes of cooking, remove the foil.
17. When cooking time is completed, open the lid and place the pan onto a wire rack to cool for about 10 minutes.

18. Carefully invert the bread onto the wire rack to cool completely before slicing.
19. Cut the bread into desired-sized slices and serve.

Serving Suggestions: Serve with butter.

Variation Tip: Dried cranberries can also be used instead of raisins.

Nutritional Information per Serving:

Calories: 441 | **Fat:** 20.3g|**Sat Fat:** 2.2g|**Carbohydrates:** 57.6g|**Fiber:** 5.7g|**Sugar:** 23.7g|**Protein:** 9.2g

Snacks & Appetizer Recipes

Roasted Cashews

Preparation Time: 5 minutes
Cooking Time: 5 minutes
Servings: 6

Ingredients:

- 1½ cups raw cashew nuts
- 1 teaspoon butter, melted
- Salt and freshly ground black pepper, as required

Preparation:

1. In a bowl, mix together all the ingredients.
2. Press "Power Button" of Ninja Foodi Digital Air Fry Oven and turn the dial to select "Air Fry" mode.
3. Press "Time Button" and again turn the dial to set the cooking time to 5 minutes.
4. Now push "Temp Button" and rotate the dial to set the temperature at 355 degrees F.
5. Press "Start/Pause" button to start.
6. When the unit beeps to show that it is preheated, open the lid.
7. Arrange the cashews into the air fry basket and insert in the oven.
8. When cooking time is completed, open the lid and
9. Shake the cashews once halfway through.
10. When cooking time is completed, open the lid and transfer the cashews into a heatproof bowl.
11. Serve warm.

Serving Suggestions: Serve with a sprinkling of little salt.

Variation Tip: Make sure to use raw walnuts.

Nutritional Information per Serving:

Calories: 202 | **Fat:** 16.5g|**Sat Fat:** 3.5g|**Carbohydrates:** 11.2g|**Fiber:** 1g|**Sugar:** 1.7g|**Protein:** 5.3g

Spicy Carrot Fries

Preparation Time: 10 minutes
Cooking Time: 12 minutes
Servings: 2

Ingredients:

- 1 large carrot, peeled and cut into sticks
- 1 tablespoon fresh rosemary, chopped finely
- 1 tablespoon olive oil
- ¼ teaspoon cayenne pepper
- Salt and ground black pepper, as required

Preparation:

1. In a bowl, add all the ingredients and mix well.
2. Press "Power Button" of Ninja Foodi Digital Air Fry Oven and turn the dial to select "Air Fry" mode.
3. Press "Time Button" and again turn the dial to set the cooking time to 12 minutes.
4. Now push "Temp Button" and rotate the dial to set the temperature at 390 degrees F.
5. Press "Start/Pause" button to start.
6. When the unit beeps to show that it is preheated, open the lid.
7. Arrange the carrot fries into the air fry basket and insert in the oven.
8. When cooking time is completed, open the lid and transfer the carrot fries onto a platter.
9. Serve warm.

Serving Suggestions: Serve with mustard sauce.

Variation Tip: You can add the spices of your choice.

Nutritional Information per Serving:

Calories: 81 | **Fat:** 8.3g|**Sat Fat:** 1.1g|**Carbohydrates:** 4.7g|**Fiber:** 1.7g|**Sugar:** 1.8g|**Protein:** 0.4g

Crispy Avocado Fries

Preparation Time: 15 minutes
Cooking Time: 7 minutes
Servings: 2

Ingredients:

- ¼ cup all-purpose flour
- Salt and ground black pepper, as required
- 1 egg
- 1 teaspoon water
- ½ cup panko breadcrumbs
- 1 avocado, peeled, pitted and sliced into 8 pieces
- Non-stick cooking spray

Preparation:

1. In a shallow bowl, mix together the flour, salt, and black pepper.
2. In a second bowl, mix well egg and water.
3. In a third bowl, put the breadcrumbs.
4. Coat the avocado slices with flour mixture, then dip into egg mixture and finally, coat evenly with the breadcrumbs.
5. Now, spray the avocado slices evenly with cooking spray.
6. Press "Power Button" of Ninja Foodi Digital Air Fry Oven and turn the dial to select "Air Fry" mode.
7. Press "Time Button" and again turn the dial to set the cooking time to 7 minutes.
8. Now push "Temp Button" and rotate the dial to set the temperature at 400 degrees F.
9. Press "Start/Pause" button to start.
10. When the unit beeps to show that it is preheated, open the lid.
11. Arrange the avocado fries into the air fry basket and insert in the oven.
12. When cooking time is completed, open the lid and transfer the avocado fries onto a platter.
13. Serve warm.

Serving Suggestions: Serve with ketchup.

Variation Tip: Make sure to use firm avocados that are not too ripe.

Nutritional Information per Serving:

Calories: 391 | **Fat:** 23.8g|**Sat Fat:** 5.6g|**Carbohydrates:** 24.8g|**Fiber:** 7.3g|**Sugar:** 0.8g|**Protein:** 7g

Beet Chips

Preparation Time: 10 minutes
Cooking Time: 15 minutes
Servings: 6

Ingredients:

- 4 medium beetroots, peeled and thinly sliced
- 2 tablespoons olive oil
- ¼ teaspoon smoked paprika
- Salt, to taste

Preparation:

1. In a large bowl and mix together all the ingredients.
2. Press "Power Button" of Ninja Foodi Digital Air Fry Oven and turn the dial to select "Air Fry" mode.
3. Press "Time Button" and again turn the dial to set the cooking time to 15 minutes.
4. Now push "Temp Button" and rotate the dial to set the temperature at 325 degrees F.
5. Press "Start/Pause" button to start.
6. When the unit beeps to show that it is preheated, open the lid.
7. Arrange the apple chips into the air fry basket and insert in the oven.
8. Toss the beet chips once halfway through.
9. When cooking time is completed, open the lid and transfer the beet chips onto a platter.
10. Serve at room temperature.

Serving Suggestions: Serve with a sprinkling of cinnamon.

Variation Tip: for a beautiful presentation, use colorful beets.

Nutritional Information per Serving:

Calories: 70 | **Fat:** 4.8g|**Sat Fat:** 0.7g|**Carbohydrates:** 6.7g|**Fiber:** 1.4g|**Sugar:** 5.3g|**Protein:** 1.1g

Cheesy Broccoli Bites

Preparation Time: 15 minutes
Cooking Time: 12 minutes
Servings: 5

Ingredients:

- 1 cup broccoli florets
- 1 egg, beaten
- ¾ cup cheddar cheese, grated
- 2 tablespoons Parmesan cheese, grated
- ¾ cup panko breadcrumbs
- Salt and freshly ground black pepper, as needed

Preparation:

1. In a food processor, add the broccoli and pulse until finely crumbled.
2. In a large bowl, mix together the broccoli and remaining ingredients.
3. Make small equal-sized balls from the mixture.
4. Press "Power Button" of Ninja Foodi Digital Air Fry Oven and turn the dial to select "Air Fry" mode.
5. Press "Time Button" and again turn the dial to set the cooking time to 12 minutes.
6. Now push "Temp Button" and rotate the dial to set the temperature at 350 degrees F.
7. Press "Start/Pause" button to start.
8. When the unit beeps to show that it is preheated, open the lid.
9. Arrange the broccoli balls into the air fry basket and insert in the oven.
10. When cooking time is completed, open the lid and transfer the broccoli bites onto a platter.
11. Serve warm.

Serving Suggestions: Serve with your favorite dipping sauce.

Variation Tip: You can use cheese of your choice.

Nutritional Information per Serving:

Calories: 153 | **Fat:** .2g|**Sat Fat:** 4.5g|**Carbohydrates:** 4g|**Fiber:** 0.5g|**Sugar:** 0.5g|**Protein:** 7.1g

Risotto Bites

Preparation Time: 15 minutes
Cooking Time: 10 minutes
Servings: 4

Ingredients:

- 1½ cups cooked risotto
- 3 tablespoons Parmesan cheese, grated
- ½ egg, beaten
- 1½ ounces mozzarella cheese, cubed
- 1/3 cup breadcrumbs

Preparation:

1. In a bowl, add the risotto, Parmesan and egg and mix until well combined.
2. Make 20 equal-sized balls from the mixture.
3. Insert a mozzarella cube in the center of each ball.
4. With your fingers smooth the risotto mixture to cover the ball.
5. In a shallow dish, place the breadcrumbs.
6. Coat the balls with the breadcrumbs evenly.
7. Press "Power Button" of Ninja Foodi Digital Air Fry Oven and turn the dial to select "Air Fry" mode.
8. Press "Time Button" and again turn the dial to set the cooking time to 10 minutes.
9. Now push "Temp Button" and rotate the dial to set the temperature at 390 degrees F.
10. Press "Start/Pause" button to start.
11. When the unit beeps to show that it is preheated, open the lid.
12. Arrange the balls into the air fry basket and insert in the oven.
13. When cooking time is completed, open the lid and transfer the risotto bites onto a platter.
14. Serve warm.

Serving Suggestions: Serve with blue cheese dip.

Variation Tip: Make sure to use dry breadcrumbs.

Nutritional Information per Serving:

Calories: 340 | **Fat:** 4.3g|**Sat Fat:** 2g|**Carbohydrates:** 62.4g|**Fiber:** 1.3g|**Sugar:** 0.7g|**Protein:** 11.3g

Buttermilk Biscuits

Preparation Time: 15 minutes
Cooking Time: 8 minutes
Servings: 8
Ingredients:

- ½ cup cake flour
- 1¼ cups all-purpose flour
- ¼ teaspoon baking soda
- ½ teaspoon baking powder
- 1 teaspoon granulated sugar
- Salt, to taste
- ¼ cup cold unsalted butter, cut into cubes
- ¾ cup buttermilk
- 2 tablespoons butter, melted

Preparation:

1. In a large bowl, sift together flours, baking soda, baking powder, sugar and salt.
2. With a pastry cutter, cut cold butter and mix until coarse crumb forms.
3. Slowly, add buttermilk and mix until a smooth dough forms.
4. Place the dough onto a floured surface and with your hands, press it into ½ inch thickness.
5. With a 1¾-inch round cookie cutter, cut the biscuits.
6. Arrange the biscuits into a baking pan in a single layer and coat with the butter.
7. Press "Power Button" of Ninja Foodi Digital Air Fry Oven and turn the dial to select "Air Fry" mode.
8. Press "Time Button" and again turn the dial to set the cooking time to 8 minutes.
9. Now push "Temp Button" and rotate the dial to set the temperature at 400 degrees F.
10. Press "Start/Pause" button to start.
11. When the unit beeps to show that it is preheated, open the lid.
12. Arrange pan over the wire rack and insert in the oven.
13. When cooking time is completed, open the lid and place the baking pan onto a wire rack for about 5 minutes.
14. Carefully invert the biscuits onto the wire rack to cool completely before serving.

Serving Suggestions: Serve with the drizzling of melted butter.

Variation Tip: Shortening can also be used instead of butter.

Nutritional Information per Serving:

Calories: 187 | **Fat:** 9.1g|**Sat Fat:** 5.6g|**Carbohydrates:** 22.6g|**Fiber:** 0.8g|**Sugar:** 1.7g|**Protein:** 3.7g

Crispy Prawns

Preparation Time: 15 minutes
Cooking Time: 8 minutes
Servings: 4

Ingredients:

- 1 egg
- ½ pound nacho chips, crushed
- 12 prawns, peeled and deveined

Preparation:

1. In a shallow dish, beat the egg.
2. In another shallow dish, place the crushed nacho chips.
3. Coat the prawn into egg and then roll into nacho chips.
4. Press "Power Button" of Ninja Foodi Digital Air Fry Oven and turn the dial to select "Air Fry" mode.
5. Press "Time Button" and again turn the dial to set the cooking time to 8 minutes.
6. Now push "Temp Button" and rotate the dial to set the temperature at 355 degrees F.
7. Press "Start/Pause" button to start.
8. When the unit beeps to show that it is preheated, open the lid.
9. Arrange the prawns into the air fry basket and insert in the oven.
10. When cooking time is completed, open the lid and serve immediately.

Serving Suggestions: Serve alongside your favorite dip.

Variation Tip: Make sure to pat dry the shrimp thoroughly before applying the coating.

Nutritional Information per Serving:

Calories: 386 | **Fat:** 17g|**Sat Fat:** 2.9g|**Carbohydrates:** 36.1g|**Fiber:** 2.6g|**Sugar:** 2.2g|**Protein:** 21g

Chicken & Parmesan Nuggets

Preparation Time: 15 minutes
Cooking Time: 10 minutes
Servings: 6

Ingredients:

- 2 large chicken breasts, cut into 1-inch cubes
- 1 cup breadcrumbs
- 1/3 tablespoon Parmesan cheese, shredded
- 1 teaspoon onion powder
- ¼ teaspoon smoked paprika
- Salt and ground black pepper, as required

Preparation:

1. In a large resealable bag, add all the ingredients.
2. Seal the bag and shake well to coat completely.
3. Press "Power Button" of Ninja Foodi Digital Air Fry Oven and turn the dial to select "Air Fry" mode.
4. Press "Time Button" and again turn the dial to set the cooking time to 10 minutes.
5. Now push "Temp Button" and rotate the dial to set the temperature at 400 degrees F.
6. Press "Start/Pause" button to start.
7. When the unit beeps to show that it is preheated, open the lid.
8. Arrange the nuggets into the air fry basket and insert in the oven.
9. When cooking time is completed, open the lid and transfer the nuggets onto a platter.
10. Serve warm.

Serving Suggestions: Serve with mustard sauce.

Variation Tip: Prefer to use freshly grated cheese.

Nutritional Information per Serving:

Calories: 218 | **Fat:** 6.6g|**Sat Fat:** 1.8g|**Carbohydrates:** 13.3g|**Fiber:** 0.9g|**Sugar:** 1.3g|**Protein:** 24.4g

Potato Bread Rolls

Preparation Time: 20 minutes
Cooking Time: 33 minutes
Servings: 8

Ingredients:

- 5 large potatoes, peeled
- 2 tablespoons vegetable oil, divided
- 2 small onions, finely chopped
- 2 green chilies, seeded and chopped
- 2 curry leaves
- ½ teaspoon ground turmeric
- Salt, as required
- 8 bread slices, trimmed

Preparation:

1. In a pan of boiling water, add the potatoes and cook for about 15-20 minutes.
2. Drain the potatoes well and with a potato masher, mash the potatoes.
3. In a skillet, heat 1 teaspoon of oil over medium heat and sauté the onion for about 4-5 minutes.
4. Add the green chilies, curry leaves, and turmeric and sauté for about 1 minute.
5. Add the mashed potatoes and salt and mix well.
6. Remove from the heat and set aside to cool completely.
7. Make 8 equal-sized oval-shaped patties from the mixture.
8. Wet the bread slices completely with water.
9. Press each bread slice between your hands to remove the excess water.
10. Place 1 bread slice in your palm and place 1 patty in the center.
11. Roll the bread slice in a spindle shape and seal the edges to secure the filling.
12. Coat the roll with some oil.
13. Repeat with the remaining slices, filling and oil.

14. Press "Power Button" of Ninja Foodi Digital Air Fry Oven and turn the dial to select "Air Fry" mode.
15. Press "Time Button" and again turn the dial to set the cooking time to 13 minutes.
16. Now push "Temp Button" and rotate the dial to set the temperature at 390 degrees F.
17. Press "Start/Pause" button to start.
18. When the unit beeps to show that it is preheated, open the lid.
19. Arrange the bread rolls into the air fry basket and insert in the oven.
20. When cooking time is completed, open the lid and transfer the rolls onto a platter.
21. Serve warm.

Serving Suggestions: Serve alongside the ketchup.

Variation Tip: Remove the moisture from bread slices completely.

Nutritional Information per Serving:

Calories: 222 | **Fat:** 4g|**Sat Fat:** 0.8g|**Carbohydrates:** 42.5g|**Fiber:** 6.2g|**Sugar:** 3.8g|**Protein:** 4.8g

Vegetables & Sides Recipes

Veggies Stuffed Bell Peppers

Preparation Time: 20 minutes
Cooking Time: 25 minutes
Servings: 6
Ingredients:

- 6 large bell peppers
- 1 bread roll, finely chopped
- 1 carrot, peeled and finely chopped
- 1 onion, finely chopped
- 1 potato, peeled and finely chopped
- ½ cup fresh peas, shelled
- 2 garlic cloves, minced
- 2 teaspoons fresh parsley, chopped
- Salt and ground black pepper, as required
- 1/3 cup cheddar cheese, grated

Preparation:

1. Remove the tops of each bell pepper and discard the seeds.
2. Chop the bell pepper tops finely.
3. In a bowl, place bell pepper tops, bread loaf, vegetables, garlic, parsley, salt and black pepper and mix well.
4. Stuff each bell pepper with the vegetable mixture.
5. Press "Power Button" of Ninja Foodi Digital Air Fry Oven and turn the dial to select "Air Fry" mode.
6. Press "Time Button" and again turn the dial to set the cooking time to 25 minutes.
7. Now push "Temp Button" and rotate the dial to set the temperature at 330 degrees F.
8. Press "Start/Pause" button to start.
9. When the unit beeps to show that it is preheated, open the lid.
10. Arrange the bell peppers into the greased air fry basket and insert in the oven.
11. After 20 minutes, sprinkle each bell pepper with cheddar cheese.
12. When cooking time is completed, open the lid and transfer the bell peppers onto serving plates.
13. Serve hot.

Serving Suggestions: Serve with fresh salad.

Variation Tip: for best result, remove the seeds from bell peppers completely.

Nutritional Information per Serving:

Calories: 123 | **Fat:** 2.7g|**Sat Fat:** 1.2g|**Carbohydrates:** 21.7g|**Fiber:** 3.7g|**Sugar:** 8g|**Protein:** 4.8g

Stuffed Eggplants

Preparation Time: 20 minutes
Cooking Time: 11 minutes
Servings: 4

Ingredients:

- 4 small eggplants, halved lengthwise
- 1 teaspoon fresh lime juice
- 1 teaspoon vegetable oil
- 1 small onion, chopped
- ¼ teaspoon garlic, chopped
- ½ of small tomato, chopped
- Salt and ground black pepper, as required
- 1 tablespoon cottage cheese, chopped
- ¼ of green bell pepper, seeded and chopped
- 1 tablespoon tomato paste
- 1 tablespoon fresh cilantro, chopped

Preparation:

1. Carefully cut a slice from one side of each eggplant lengthwise.
2. With a small spoon, scoop out the flesh from each eggplant, leaving a thick shell.
3. Transfer the eggplant flesh into a bowl.
4. Drizzle the eggplants with lime juice evenly.
5. Press "Power Button" of Ninja Foodi Digital Air Fry Oven and turn the dial to select "Air Fry" mode.
6. Press "Time Button" and again turn the dial to set the cooking time to 3 minutes.
7. Now push "Temp Button" and rotate the dial to set the temperature at 320 degrees F.
8. Press "Start/Pause" button to start.
9. When the unit beeps to show that it is preheated, open the lid.
10. Arrange the hollowed eggplants into the greased air fry basket and insert in the oven.
11. Meanwhile, in a skillet, heat the oil over medium heat and sauté the onion and garlic for about 2 minutes.
12. Add the eggplant flesh, tomato, salt, and black pepper and sauté for about 2 minutes.
13. Stir in the cheese, bell pepper, tomato paste, and cilantro and cook for about 1 minute.
14. Remove the pan of the veggie mixture from heat.

15. When the cooking time is completed, open the lid and arrange the cooked eggplants onto a plate.
16. Stuff each eggplant with the veggie mixture.
17. Close each with its cut part.
18. Again arrange the eggplants shells into the greased air fry basket and insert into the oven.
19. Press "Power Button" of Ninja Foodi Digital Air Fry Oven and turn the dial to select "Air Fry" mode.
20. Press "Time Button" and again turn the dial to set the cooking time to 8 minutes.
21. Now push "Temp Button" and rotate the dial to set the temperature at 320 degrees F.
22. Press "Start/Pause" button to start.
23. When cooking time is completed, open the lid and transfer the eggplants onto serving plates.
24. Serve hot.

Serving Suggestions: Serve with the topping f feta cheese.

Variation Tip: Clean the eggplant by running under cold running water.

Nutritional Information per Serving:

Calories: 131 | **Fat:** 2g|**Sat Fat:** 0.3g|**Carbohydrates:** 27.8g|**Fiber:** 5.3g|**Sugar:** 4.3g|**Protein:** 5.1g

Pita Bread Pizza

Preparation Time: 10 minutes
Cooking Time: 5 minutes
Servings: 1
Ingredients:

- 2 tablespoons marinara sauce
- 1 whole-wheat pita bread
- ½ cup fresh baby spinach leaves
- ½ of small plum tomato, cut into 4 slices
- ½ of garlic clove, sliced thinly
- ½ ounce part-skim mozzarella cheese, shredded
- ½ tablespoon Parmigiano-Reggiano cheese, shredded

Preparation:

1. Arrange the pita bread onto a plate.
2. Spread marinara sauce over 1 side of each pita bread evenly.
3. Top with the spinach leaves, followed by tomato slices, garlic and cheeses.
4. Press "Power Button" of Ninja Foodi Digital Air Fry Oven and turn the dial to select "Air Fry" mode.
5. Press "Time Button" and again turn the dial to set the cooking time to 5 minutes.
6. Now push "Temp Button" and rotate the dial to set the temperature at 350 degrees F.
7. Press "Start/Pause" button to start.
8. When the unit beeps to show that it is preheated, open the lid.
9. Arrange the pita bread into the greased air fry basket and insert in the oven.
10. When cooking time is completed, open the lid and transfer the pizza onto a serving plate.
11. Set aside to cool slightly.
12. Serve warm.

Serving Suggestions: Serve alongside the greens.

Variation Tip: You can replace pizza sauce with marinara sauce.

Nutritional Information per Serving:

Calories: 266 | **Fat:** 6.2g|**Sat Fat:** 2.6g|**Carbohydrates:** 43.1g|**Fiber:** 6.5g|**Sugar:** 4.6g|**Protein:** 13g

Quinoa Burgers

Preparation Time: 10 minutes
Cooking Time: 10 minutes
Servings: 4

Ingredients:

- ½ cup cooked and cooled quinoa
- 1 cup rolled oats
- 2 eggs, lightly beaten
- ¼ cup white onion, minced
- ¼ cup feta cheese, crumbled
- Salt and ground black pepper, as required
- Olive oil cooking spray

Preparation:

1. In a large bowl, add all ingredients and mix until well combined.
2. Make 4 equal-sized patties from the mixture.
3. Lightly spray the patties with cooking spray.
4. Press "Power Button" of Ninja Foodi Digital Air Fry Oven and turn the dial to select "Air Fry" mode.
5. Press "Time Button" and again turn the dial to set the cooking time to 10 minutes.
6. Now push "Temp Button" and rotate the dial to set the temperature at 400 degrees F.
7. Press "Start/Pause" button to start.
8. When the unit beeps to show that it is preheated, open the lid.
9. Arrange the patties into the greased air fry basket and insert in the oven.
10. Flip the patties once halfway through.
11. When cooking time is completed, open the lid and transfer the patties onto a platter.
12. Serve warm.

Serving Suggestions: Serve with green sauce.

Variation Tip: For crispy texture, refrigerate the patties for at least 15 minutes before cooking.

Nutritional Information per Serving:

Calories: 215 | **Fat:** 6.6g|**Sat Fat:** 2.5g|**Carbohydrates:** 28.7g|**Fiber:** 3.7g|**Sugar:** 1.1g|**Protein:** 9.9g

Tofu with Broccoli

Preparation Time: 15 minutes
Cooking Time: 15 minutes
Servings: 2

Ingredients:

- 8 ounces block firm tofu, pressed and cubed
- 1 small head broccoli, cut into florets
- 1 tablespoon canola oil
- 1 tablespoon nutritional yeast
- ¼ teaspoon dried parsley
- Salt and ground black pepper, as required

Preparation:

1. In a bowl, mix together the tofu, broccoli and the remaining ingredients.
2. Press "Power Button" of Ninja Foodi Digital Air Fry Oven and turn the dial to select "Air Fry" mode.
3. Press "Time Button" and again turn the dial to set the cooking time to 15 minutes.
4. Now push "Temp Button" and rotate the dial to set the temperature at 390 degrees F.
5. Press "Start/Pause" button to start.
6. When the unit beeps to show that it is preheated, open the lid.
7. Arrange the tofu mixture into the greased air fry basket and insert in the oven.
8. Flip the tofu mixture once halfway through.
9. When cooking time is completed, open the lid and serve hot.

Serving Suggestions: Serve with the garnishing of sesame seeds.

Variation Tip: Cut the broccoli in small florets.

Nutritional Information per Serving:

Calories: 206 | **Fat:** 13.1g|**Sat Fat:** 1.6g|**Carbohydrates:** 12.1g|**Fiber:** 5.4g|**Sugar:** 2.6g|**Protein:** 15g

Sweet & Spicy Parsnips

Preparation Time: 15 minutes
Cooking Time: 44 minutes
Servings: 5

Ingredients:

- 1½ pound parsnip, peeled and cut into 1-inch chunks
- 1 tablespoon butter, melted
- 2 tablespoons honey
- 1 tablespoon dried parsley flakes, crushed
- ¼ teaspoon red pepper flakes, crushed
- Salt and ground black pepper, as required

Preparation:

1. In a large bowl, mix together the parsnips and butter.
2. Press "Power Button" of Ninja Foodi Digital Air Fry Oven and turn the dial to select "Air Fry" mode.
3. Press "Time Button" and again turn the dial to set the cooking time to 44 minutes.
4. Now push "Temp Button" and rotate the dial to set the temperature at 355 degrees F.
5. Press "Start/Pause" button to start.
6. When the unit beeps to show that it is preheated, open the lid.
7. Arrange the squash chunks into the greased air fry basket and insert in the oven.
8. Meanwhile, in another large bowl, mix together the remaining ingredients.
9. After 40 minutes of cooking, press "Start/Pause" button to pause the unit.
10. Transfer the parsnips chunks into the bowl of honey mixture and toss to coat well.
11. Again, arrange the parsnip chunks into the air fry basket and insert in the oven.
12. When cooking time is completed, open the lid and serve hot.

Serving Suggestions: Serve with garlic bread.

Variation Tip: Make sure to cut the parsnip into uniform-sized chunks.

Nutritional Information per Serving:

Calories: 149 | **Fat:** 2.7g|**Sat Fat:** 1.5g|**Carbohydrates:** 31.5g|**Fiber:** 6.7g|**Sugar:** 13.5g|**Protein:** 1.7g

Cauliflower in Buffalo Sauce

Preparation Time: 10 minutes
Cooking Time: 12 minutes
Servings: 4

Ingredients:

- 1 large head cauliflower, cut into bite-size florets
- 1 tablespoon olive oil
- 2 teaspoons garlic powder
- Salt and ground black pepper, as required
- 1 tablespoon butter, melted
- 2/3 cup warm buffalo sauce

Preparation:

1. In a large bowl, add cauliflower florets, olive oil, garlic powder, salt and pepper and toss to coat.
2. Press "Power Button" of Ninja Foodi Digital Air Fry Oven and turn the dial to select "Air Fry" mode.
3. Press "Time Button" and again turn the dial to set the cooking time to 12 minutes.
4. Now push "Temp Button" and rotate the dial to set the temperature at 375 degrees F.
5. Press "Start/Pause" button to start.
6. When the unit beeps to show that it is preheated, open the lid.
7. Arrange the cauliflower florets in the air fry basket and insert in the oven.
8. After 7 minutes of cooking, coat the cauliflower florets with buffalo sauce.
9. When cooking time is completed, open the lid and serve hot.

Serving Suggestions: Serve with the garnishing of scallions.

Variation Tip: Use best quality buffalo sauce.

Nutritional Information per Serving:

Calories: 183 | **Fat:** 17.1g|**Sat Fat:** 4.3g|**Carbohydrates:** 5.9g|**Fiber:** 1.8g|**Sugar:** 1.0g|**Protein:** 1.6g

Broccoli with Cauliflower

Preparation Time: 15 minutes
Cooking Time: 20 minutes
Servings: 4

Ingredients:

- 1½ cups broccoli, cut into 1-inch pieces
- 1½ cups cauliflower, cut into 1-inch pieces
- 1 tablespoon olive oil
- Salt, as required

Preparation:

1. In a bowl, add the vegetables, oil, and salt and toss to coat well.
2. Press "Power Button" of Ninja Foodi Digital Air Fry Oven and turn the dial to select "Air Fry" mode.
3. Press "Time Button" and again turn the dial to set the cooking time to 20 minutes.
4. Now push "Temp Button" and rotate the dial to set the temperature at 375 degrees F.
5. Press "Start/Pause" button to start.
6. When the unit beeps to show that it is preheated, open the lid.
7. Arrange the veggie mixture into the greased air fry basket and insert in the oven.
8. When cooking time is completed, open the lid and serve hot.

Serving Suggestions: Serve with the drizzling of lemon juice.

Variation Tip: You can add spices according to your taste.

Nutritional Information per Serving:

Calories: 51 | **Fat:** 3.7g|**Sat Fat:** 0.5g|**Carbohydrates:** 4.3g|**Fiber:** 1.8g|**Sugar:** 1.5g|**Protein:** 1.7g

Vinegar Green Beans

Preparation Time: 10 minutes
Cooking Time: 20 minutes
Servings: 2

Ingredients:

- 1 (10-ounce) bag frozen cut green beans
- ¼ cup nutritional yeast
- 3 tablespoons balsamic vinegar
- Salt and ground black pepper, as required

Preparation:

1. In a bowl, add the green beans, nutritional yeast, vinegar, salt, and black pepper and toss to coat well.
2. Press "Power Button" of Ninja Foodi Digital Air Fry Oven and turn the dial to select "Air Fry" mode.
3. Press "Time Button" and again turn the dial to set the cooking time to 20 minutes.
4. Now push "Temp Button" and rotate the dial to set the temperature at 400 degrees F.
5. Press "Start/Pause" button to start.
6. When the unit beeps to show that it is preheated, open the lid.
7. Arrange the green beans into the greased air fry basket and insert in the oven.
8. When cooking time is completed, open the lid and serve hot.

Serving Suggestions: Serve with the garnishing of sesame seeds.

Variation Tip: Balsamic vinegar can be replaced with lemon juice.

Nutritional Information per Serving:

Calories: 115 | **Fat:** 1.3g|**Sat Fat:** 0.2g|**Carbohydrates:** 18.5g|**Fiber:** 9.3g|**Sugar:** 1.8g|**Protein:** 11.3g

Herbed Bell Peppers

Preparation Time: 10 minutes
Cooking Time: 8 minutes
Servings: 4

Ingredients:

- 1½ pounds mixed bell peppers, seeded and sliced
- 1 small onion, sliced
- ½ teaspoon dried thyme, crushed
- ½ teaspoon dried savory, crushed
- Salt and ground black pepper, as required
- 2 tablespoon butter, melted

Preparation:

1. In a bowl, add the bell peppers, onion, herbs, salt and black pepper and toss to coat well.
2. Press "Power Button" of Ninja Foodi Digital Air Fry Oven and turn the dial to select "Air Fry" mode.
3. Press "Time Button" and again turn the dial to set the cooking time to 8 minutes.
4. Now push "Temp Button" and rotate the dial to set the temperature at 360 degrees F.
5. Press "Start/Pause" button to start.
6. When the unit beeps to show that it is preheated, open the lid.
7. Arrange the bell peppers into the air fry basket and insert in the oven.
8. When cooking time is completed, open the lid and transfer the bell peppers into a bowl.
9. Drizzle with butter and serve immediately.

Serving Suggestions: Serve with boiled rice.

Variation Tip: Feel free to use herbs of your choice.

Nutritional Information per Serving:

Calories: 73 | **Fat:** 5.9g|**Sat Fat:** 3.7g|**Carbohydrates:** 5.2g|**Fiber:** 1.1g|**Sugar:** 3g|**Protein:** 0.7g

Fish & Seafood Recipes

Spicy Salmon

Preparation Time: 10 minutes
Cooking Time: 11 minutes
Servings: 2

Ingredients:

- 1 teaspoon smoked paprika
- 1 teaspoon cayenne pepper
- 1 teaspoon onion powder
- 1 teaspoon garlic powder
- Salt and ground black pepper, as required
- 2 (6-ounce) (1½-inch thick) salmon fillets
- 2 teaspoons olive oil

Preparation:

1. Add the spices in a bowl and mix well.
2. Drizzle the salmon fillets with oil and then rub with the spice mixture.
3. Press "Power Button" of Ninja Foodi Digital Air Fry Oven and turn the dial to select "Air Fry" mode.
4. Press "Time Button" and again turn the dial to set the cooking time to 11 minutes.
5. Now push "Temp Button" and rotate the dial to set the temperature at 390 degrees F.
6. Press "Start/Pause" button to start.
7. When the unit beeps to show that it is preheated, open the lid.
8. Arrange the salmon fillets into the greased air fry basket and insert in the oven.
9. When cooking time is completed, open the lid and serve hot.

Serving Suggestions: Serve with your favorite salad.

Variation Tip: Adjust the ratio of spices according to your taste.

Nutritional Information per Serving:

Calories: 280 | **Fat:** 15.5g|**Sat Fat:** 2.2g|**Carbohydrates:** 3.1g|**Fiber:** 0.8g|**Sugar:** 1g|**Protein:** 33.6g

Lemony Salmon

Preparation Time: 10 minutes
Cooking Time: 8 minutes
Servings: 3

Ingredients:

- 1½ pounds salmon
- ½ teaspoon red chili powder
- Salt and ground black pepper, as required
- 1 lemon, cut into slices
- 1 tablespoon fresh dill, chopped

Preparation:

1. Season the salmon with chili powder, salt, and black pepper.
2. Press "Power Button" of Ninja Foodi Digital Air Fry Oven and turn the dial to select "Air Fry" mode.
3. Press "Time Button" and again turn the dial to set the cooking time to 8 minutes.
4. Now push "Temp Button" and rotate the dial to set the temperature at 375 degrees F.
5. Press "Start/Pause" button to start.
6. When the unit beeps to show that it is preheated, open the lid.
7. Arrange the salmon fillets into the greased air fry basket and insert in the oven.
8. When cooking time is completed, open the lid and serve hot with the garnishing of fresh dill.

Serving Suggestions: Serve with the topping of cheese.

Variation Tip: Make sure to pat dry the salmon completely before seasoning.

Nutritional Information per Serving:

Calories: 305 | **Fat:** 14.1g|**Sat Fat:** 2g|**Carbohydrates:** 1.3g|**Fiber:** 0.4g|**Sugar:** 0.2g|**Protein:** 44.3g

Salmon & Asparagus Parcel

Preparation Time: 15 minutes
Cooking Time: 13 minutes
Servings: 2

Ingredients:

- 2 (4-ounce) salmon fillets
- 6 asparagus stalks
- ¼ cup white sauce
- 1 teaspoon oil
- ¼ cup champagne
- Salt and ground black pepper, as required

Preparation:

1. In a bowl, mix together all the ingredients.
2. Divide the salmon mixture over 2 pieces of foil evenly.
3. Seal the foil around the salmon mixture to form the packet.
4. Press "Power Button" of Ninja Foodi Digital Air Fry Oven and turn the dial to select "Air Fry" mode.
5. Press "Time Button" and again turn the dial to set the cooking time to 13 minutes.
6. Now push "Temp Button" and rotate the dial to set the temperature at 355 degrees F.
7. Press "Start/Pause" button to start.
8. When the unit beeps to show that it is preheated, open the lid.
9. Arrange the salmon parcels into the air fry basket and insert in the oven.
10. When cooking time is completed, open the lid and serve hot.

Serving Suggestions: Serve with the garnishing of fresh herbs.

Variation Tip: Don't overcook the salmon.

Nutritional Information per Serving:

Calories: 243 | **Fat:** 12.7g|**Sat Fat:** 2.2g|**Carbohydrates:** 9.4g|**Fiber:** 1.8g|**Sugar:** 6g|**Protein:** 25g

Salmon with Broccoli

Preparation Time: 15 minutes
Cooking Time: 12 minutes
Servings: 2

Ingredients:

- 1½ cups small broccoli florets
- 2 tablespoons vegetable oil, divided
- Salt and ground black pepper, as required
- 1 (½-inch) piece fresh ginger, grated
- 1 tablespoon soy sauce
- 1 teaspoon rice vinegar
- 1 teaspoon light brown sugar
- ¼ teaspoon cornstarch
- 2 (6-ounce) skin-on salmon fillets
- 1 scallion, thinly sliced

Preparation:

1. In a bowl, mix together the broccoli, 1 tablespoon of oil, salt, and black pepper.
2. In another bowl, mix well the ginger, soy sauce, vinegar, sugar, and cornstarch.
3. Coat the salmon fillets with remaining oil and then with the ginger mixture.
4. Press "Power Button" of Ninja Foodi Digital Air Fry Oven and turn the dial to select "Air Fry" mode.
5. Press "Time Button" and again turn the dial to set the cooking time to 12 minutes.
6. Now push "Temp Button" and rotate the dial to set the temperature at 375 degrees F.
7. Press "Start/Pause" button to start.
8. When the unit beeps to show that it is preheated, open the lid.
9. Arrange the broccoli florets into the greased air fry basket and top with the salmon fillets.
10. Insert the basket in the oven.
11. When cooking time is completed, open the

Serving Suggestions: Serve with the garnishing of lemon zest.

Variation Tip: Use low-sodium soy sauce.

Nutritional Information per Serving:

Calories: 385 | **Fat:** 24.4g|**Sat Fat:** 4.2g|**Carbohydrates:** 7.8g|**Fiber:** 2.1g|**Sugar:** 3g|**Protein:** 35.6g

Crispy Catfish

Preparation Time: 15 minutes
Cooking Time: 15 minutes
Servings: 5
Ingredients:

- 5 (6-ounce) catfish fillets
- 1 cup milk
- 2 teaspoons fresh lemon juice
- ½ cup yellow mustard
- ½ cup cornmeal
- ¼ cup all-purpose flour
- 2 tablespoons dried parsley flakes
- ¼ teaspoon red chili powder
- ¼ teaspoon cayenne pepper
- ¼ teaspoon onion powder
- ¼ teaspoon garlic powder
- Salt and ground black pepper, as required
- Olive oil cooking spray

Preparation:

1. In a large bowl, place the catfish, milk, and lemon juice and refrigerate for about 15 minutes.
2. In a shallow bowl, add the mustard.
3. In another bowl, mix together the cornmeal, flour, parsley flakes and spices.
4. Remove the catfish fillets from milk mixture and with paper towels, pat them dry.
5. Coat each fish fillet with mustard and then roll into cornmeal mixture.
6. Then, spray each fillet with the cooking spray.
7. Press "Power Button" of Ninja Foodi Digital Air Fry Oven and turn the dial to select "Air Fry" mode.
8. Press "Time Button" and again turn the dial to set the cooking time to 15 minutes.
9. Now push "Temp Button" and rotate the dial to set the temperature at 400 degrees F.
10. Press "Start/Pause" button to start.
11. When the unit beeps to show that it is preheated, open the lid.
12. Arrange the catfish fillets into the greased air fry basket and insert in the oven.
13. After 10 minutes of cooking, flip the fillets and spray with the cooking spray.
14. When cooking time is completed, open the lid and serve hot.

Serving Suggestions: Serve with cheese sauce.

Variation Tip: Use freshly squeezed lemon juice.

Nutritional Information per Serving:

Calories: 340 | **Fat:** 15.5g|**Sat Fat:** 3.1g|**Carbohydrates:** 18.3g|**Fiber:** 2g|**Sugar:** 2.7g|**Protein:** 30.9g

Tangy Sea Bass

Preparation Time: 10 minutes
Cooking Time: 12 minutes
Servings: 2

Ingredients:

- 2 (5-ounce) sea bass fillets
- 1 garlic clove, minced
- 1 teaspoon fresh dill, minced
- 1 tablespoon olive oil
- 1 tablespoon balsamic vinegar
- Salt and ground black pepper, as required

Preparation:

1. In a large resealable bag, add all the ingredients.
2. Seal the bag and shake well to mix.
3. Refrigerate to marinate for at least 30 minutes.
4. Remove the fish fillets from bag and shake off the excess marinade.
5. Arrange the fish fillets onto the greased sheet pan in a single layer.
6. Press "Power Button" of Ninja Foodi Digital Air Fry Oven and turn the dial to select "Air Bake" mode.
7. Press "Time Button" and again turn the dial to set the cooking time to 12 minutes.
8. Now push "Temp Button" and rotate the dial to set the temperature at 450 degrees F.
9. Press "Start/Pause" button to start.
10. When the unit beeps to show that it is preheated, open the lid and insert the sheet pan in oven.
11. When cooking time is completed, open the Flip the fish fillets once halfway through.
12. When cooking time is completed, open the lid and serve hot.

Serving Suggestions: Serve with fresh salad.

Variation Tip: Rinse fish with cool, running water and pat it dry.

Nutritional Information per Serving:

Calories: 241 | **Fat:** 10.7g|**Sat Fat:** 1.9g|**Carbohydrates:** 0.9g|**Fiber:** 0.1g|**Sugar:** 0.1g|**Protein:** 33.7g

Cod with Sauce

Preparation Time: 15 minutes
Cooking Time: 15 minutes
Servings: 2

Ingredients:

- 2 (7-ounce) cod fillets
- Salt and ground black pepper, as required
- ¼ teaspoon sesame oil
- 1 cup water
- 5 little squares rock sugar
- 5 tablespoons light soy sauce
- 1 teaspoon dark soy sauce
- 2 scallions (green part), sliced
- ¼ cup fresh cilantro, chopped
- 3 tablespoons olive oil
- 5 ginger slices

Preparation:

1. Season each cod fillet evenly with salt, and black pepper and drizzle with sesame oil.
2. Set aside at room temperature for about 15-20 minutes.
3. Press "Power Button" of Ninja Foodi Digital Air Fry Oven and turn the dial to select "Air Fry" mode.
4. Press "Time Button" and again turn the dial to set the cooking time to 12 minutes.
5. Now push "Temp Button" and rotate the dial to set the temperature at 355 degrees F.
6. Press "Start/Pause" button to start.
7. When the unit beeps to show that it is preheated, open the lid.
8. Arrange the cod fillets into the greased air fry basket and insert in the oven.
9. Meanwhile, in a small pan, add the water and bring it to a boil.
10. Add the rock sugar and both soy sauces and cook until sugar is dissolved, stirring continuously.
11. Remove from the heat and set aside.
12. Remove the cod fillets from oven and transfer onto serving plates.
13. Top each fillet with scallion and cilantro.
14. In a small frying pan, heat the olive oil over medium heat and sauté the ginger slices for about 2-3 minutes.
15. Remove the frying pan from heat and discard the ginger slices.
16. When cooking time is completed, open the lid and transfer the cod fillets onto serving plates.
17. Carefully pour the hot oil evenly over cod fillets.

18. Top with the sauce mixture and serve.

Serving Suggestions: Serve with boiled rice.

Variation Tip: For best result, use toasted sesame oil.

Nutritional Information per Serving:

Calories: 380 | **Fat:** 23.4g|**Sat Fat:** 3.1g|**Carbohydrates:** 5g|**Fiber:** 0.8g|**Sugar:** 1.1g|**Protein:** 38.3g

Cod Burgers

Preparation Time: 15 minutes
Cooking Time: 7 minutes
Servings: 4

Ingredients:

- ½ pound cod fillets
- ½ teaspoon fresh lime zest, grated finely
- ½ egg
- ½ teaspoon red chili paste
- Salt, to taste
- ½ tablespoon fresh lime juice
- 3 tablespoons coconut, grated and divided
- 1 small scallion, chopped finely
- 1 tablespoon fresh parsley, chopped

Preparation:

1. In a food processor, add cod filets, lime zest, egg, chili paste, salt and lime juice and pulse until smooth.
2. Transfer the cod mixture into a bowl.
3. Add 1½ tablespoons coconut, scallion and parsley and mix until well combined.
4. Make 4 equal-sized patties from the mixture.
5. In a shallow dish, place the remaining coconut.
6. Coat the patties in coconut evenly.
7. Press "Power Button" of Ninja Foodi Digital Air Fry Oven and turn the dial to select "Air Fry" mode.
8. Press "Time Button" and again turn the dial to set the cooking time to 7 minutes.
9. Now push "Temp Button" and rotate the dial to set the temperature at 375 degrees F.
10. Press "Start/Pause" button to start.
11. When the unit beeps to show that it is preheated, open the lid.
12. Arrange the patties into the greased air fry basket and insert in the oven.
13. When cooking time is completed, open the lid and serve hot.

Serving Suggestions: Serve alongside the dipping sauce.

Variation Tip: Use unsweetened coconut.

Nutritional Information per Serving:

Calories: 70 | **Fat:** 2.4g|**Sat Fat:** 1.3g|**Carbohydrates:** 1.1g|**Fiber:** 0.4g|**Sugar:** 0.5g|**Protein:** 11g

Crab Cakes

Preparation Time: 15 minutes
Cooking Time: 10 minutes
Servings: 4

Ingredients:

- ¼ cup red bell pepper, seeded and chopped finely
- 2 scallions, chopped finely
- 2 tablespoons mayonnaise
- 2 tablespoons breadcrumbs
- 1 tablespoon Dijon mustard
- 1 teaspoon old bay seasoning
- 8 ounces lump crabmeat, drained

Preparation:

1. In a large bowl, add all the ingredients except crabmeat and mix until well combined.
2. Gently fold in the crabmeat.
3. Make 4 equal-sized patties from the mixture.
4. Arrange the patties onto the lightly greased sheet pan.
5. Press "Power Button" of Ninja Foodi Digital Air Fry Oven and turn the dial to select the "Air Fry" mode.
6. Press "Time Button" and again turn the dial to set the cooking time to 10 minutes.
7. Now push "Temp Button" and rotate the dial to set the temperature at 370 degrees F.
8. Press "Start/Pause" button to start.
9. When the unit beeps to show that it is preheated, open the lid and insert the sheet pan in oven.
10. When cooking time is completed, open the lid and serve hot.

Serving Suggestions: Serve alongside the fresh salad.

Variation Tip: Make sure to remove any cartilage from crabmeat.

Nutritional Information per Serving:

Calories: 91 | **Fat:** 7.4g|**Sat Fat:** 0.4g|**Carbohydrates:** 6.4g|**Fiber:** 0.6g|**Sugar:** 1.3g|**Protein:** 9.1g

Herbed Shrimp

Preparation Time: 15 minutes
Cooking Time: 7 minutes
Servings: 3

Ingredients:

- 4 tablespoons salted butter, melted
- 1 tablespoon fresh lemon juice
- 1 tablespoon garlic, minced
- 2 teaspoons red pepper flakes, crushed
- 1 pound shrimp, peeled and deveined
- 2 tablespoons fresh basil, chopped
- 1 tablespoon fresh chives, chopped
- 2 tablespoons chicken broth

Preparation:

1. In a 7-inch round baking pan, place butter, lemon juice, garlic, and red pepper flakes and mix well.
2. Press "Power Button" of Ninja Foodi Digital Air Fry Oven and turn the dial to select the "Air Fry" mode.
3. Press "Time Button" and again turn the dial to set the cooking time to 7 minutes.
4. Now push "Temp Button" and rotate the dial to set the temperature at 325 degrees F.
5. Press "Start/Pause" button to start.
6. When the unit beeps to show that it is preheated, open the lid and place the pan over wire rack.
7. Insert the wire rack in oven.
8. After 2 minutes of cooking in the pan, stir in the shrimp, basil, chives and broth.
9. When cooking time is completed, open the lid and stir the mixture.
10. Serve hot.

Serving Suggestions: Serve with the garnishing of scallion.

Variation Tip: Avoid shrimp that smells like ammonia.

Nutritional Information per Serving:

Calories: 327 | **Fat:** 18.3g|**Sat Fat:** 10.6g|**Carbohydrates:** 4.2g|**Fiber:** 0.5g|**Sugar:** 0.3g|**Protein:** 35.3g

Spiced Shrimp

Preparation Time: 15 minutes
Cooking Time: 5 minutes
Servings: 3

Ingredients:

- 1 pound tiger shrimp
- 3 tablespoons olive oil
- 1 teaspoon old bay seasoning
- ½ teaspoon cayenne pepper
- ½ teaspoon smoked paprika
- Salt, as required

Preparation:

1. In a large bowl, add all the ingredients and stir to combine.
2. Press "Power Button" of Ninja Foodi Digital Air Fry Oven and turn the dial to select "Air Fry" mode.
3. Press "Time Button" and again turn the dial to set the cooking time to 5 minutes.

4. Now push "Temp Button" and rotate the dial to set the temperature at 390 degrees F.
5. Press "Start/Pause" button to start.
6. When the unit beeps to show that it is preheated, open the lid.
7. Arrange the shrimp into the greased air fry basket and insert in the oven.
8. When cooking time is completed, open the lid and serve hot.

Serving Suggestions: Serve with fresh greens.

Variation Tip: You can use seasoning of your choice.

Nutritional Information per Serving:

Calories: 272 | **Fat:** 15.7g|**Sat Fat:** 2.5g|**Carbohydrates:** 0.4g|**Fiber:** 0.2g|**Sugar:** 0.1g|**Protein:** 31.7g

Salmon with Prawns

Preparation Time: 15 minutes
Cooking Time: 18 minutes
Servings: 4

Ingredients:

- 4 (4-ounce) salmon fillets
- 2 tablespoons olive oil
- ½ pound cherry tomatoes, chopped
- 8 large prawns, peeled and deveined
- 2 tablespoons fresh lemon juice
- 2 tablespoons fresh thyme, chopped

Preparation:

1. In the bottom of a greased baking pan, place salmon fillets and tomatoes in a greased baking dish in a single layer and drizzle with the oil.
2. Arrange the prawns on top in a single layer.
3. Drizzle with lemon juice and sprinkle with thyme.
4. Press "Power Button" of Ninja Foodi Digital Air Fry Oven and turn the dial to select "Air Fry" mode.
5. Press "Time Button" and again turn the dial to set the cooking time to 8 minutes.
6. Now push "Temp Button" and rotate the dial to set the temperature at 390 degrees F.
7. Press "Start/Pause" button to start.
8. When the unit beeps to show that it is preheated, open the lid.
9. Arrange the baking pan into the air fry basket and insert in the oven.
10. When cooking time is completed, open the lid and serve immediately.

Serving Suggestions: Serve with pasta of your choice.

Variation Tip: Make sure to use fresh salmon and prawns.

Nutritional Information per Serving:

Calories: 239 | **Fat:** 14.5g|**Sat Fat:** 2.2g|**Carbohydrates:** 3.4g|**Fiber:** 1.2g|**Sugar:** 1.7g|**Protein:** 25.2g

Poultry Recipes

Simple Chicken Thighs

Preparation Time: 10 minutes
Cooking Time: 20 minutes
Servings: 4

Ingredients:

- 4 (4-ounces) skinless, boneless chicken thighs
- Salt and ground black pepper, as required
- 2 tablespoons butter, melted

Preparation:

1. Line a sheet pan with a lightly greased piece of foil.
2. Rub the chicken thighs with salt and black pepper evenly and then, brush with melted butter.
3. Place the chicken thighs into the prepared sheet pan.
4. Press "Power Button" of Ninja Foodi Digital Air Fry Oven and turn the dial to select "Air Bake" mode.
5. Press "Time Button" and again turn the dial to set the cooking time to 20 minutes.
6. Now push "Temp Button" and rotate the dial to set the temperature at 450 degrees F.
7. Press "Start/Pause" button to start.
8. When the unit beeps to show that it is preheated, open the lid and insert the sheet pan in oven.
9. When the cooking time is completed, open the lid and serve hot.

Serving Suggestions: Serve alongside the creamy mashed potatoes.

Variation Tip: Pat the chicken thighs dry with a paper towel.

Nutritional Information per Serving:

Calories: 193 | **Fat:** 9.8g|**Sat Fat:** 5.2g|**Carbohydrates:** 0g|**Fiber:** 0g|**Sugar:** 0g|**Protein:** 25.4g

Herbed Whole Chicken

Preparation Time: 15 minutes
Cooking Time: 1 hour
Servings: 8

Ingredients:

- 1 tablespoon fresh basil, chopped
- 1 tablespoon fresh oregano, chopped
- 1 tablespoon fresh thyme, chopped
- Salt and ground black pepper, as required
- 1 (4½-pound) whole chicken, necks and giblets removed
- 3 tablespoons olive oil, divided

Preparation:

1. In a bowl, mix together the herbs, salt and black pepper.
2. Coat the chicken with 2 tablespoons of oil and then, rub inside, outside and underneath the skin with half of the herb mixture generously.
3. Press "Power Button" of Ninja Foodi Digital Air Fry Oven and turn the dial to select "Air Fry" mode.
4. Press "Time Button" and again turn the dial to set the cooking time to 60 minutes.
5. Now push "Temp Button" and rotate the dial to set the temperature at 360 degrees F.
6. Press "Start/Pause" button to start.
7. When the unit beeps to show that it is preheated, open the lid.
8. Arrange the chicken into the greased air fry basket, breast-side down and insert in the oven.
9. After 30 minutes of cooking, arrange the chicken, breast-side up and coat with the remaining oil.
10. Then rub with the remaining herb mixture.
11. When the cooking time is completed, open the lid and place the chicken onto a cutting board for about 10 minutes before carving.
12. With a sharp knife, cut the chicken into desired sized pieces and serve.

Serving Suggestions: Serve with roasted vegetables.

Variation Tip: Dried herbs can be used instead of fresh herbs.

Nutritional Information per Serving:

Calories: 533 | **Fat:** 24.3g|**Sat Fat:** 6g|**Carbohydrates:** 0.6g|**Fiber:** 0.4g|**Sugar:** 0g|**Protein:** 73.9g

Buttermilk Whole Chicken

Preparation Time: 15 minutes
Cooking Time: 50 minutes
Servings: 6

Ingredients:

- 2 cups buttermilk
- ¼ cup olive oil
- 1 teaspoon garlic powder
- Salt, as required
- 1 (3-pound) whole chicken, neck and giblets removed
- Ground black pepper, as required

Preparation:

1. In a large resealable bag, mix together the buttermilk, oil, garlic powder and 1 tablespoon of salt.
2. Add the whole chicken and seal the bag tightly.
3. Refrigerate to marinate for 24 hours up to 2 days.
4. Remove the chicken from bag and pat dry with paper towels.
5. Season the chicken with salt and black pepper.
6. With kitchen twine, tie off wings and legs.
7. Press "Power Button" of Ninja Foodi Digital Air Fry Oven and turn the dial to select "Air Fry" mode.
8. Press "Time Button" and again turn the dial to set the cooking time to 50 minutes.
9. Now push "Temp Button" and rotate the dial to set the temperature at 380 degrees F.
10. Press "Start/Pause" button to start.
11. When the unit beeps to show that it is preheated, open the lid.
12. Arrange the chicken into the greased air fry basket, breast-side down and insert in the oven.
13. When the cooking time is completed, open the lid and place the chicken onto a cutting board for about 10 minutes before carving.
14. With a sharp knife, cut the chicken into desired sized pieces and serve.

Serving Suggestions: Serve with steamed veggies

Variation Tip: Kitchen shears are very useful for trimming excess fat from the chicken's cavity.

Nutritional Information per Serving:

Calories: 449 | **Fat:** 16g|**Sat Fat:** 3.6g|**Carbohydrates:** 68.5g|**Fiber:** 4.3g|**Sugar:** 0.1g|**Protein:** 4g

Crispy Roasted Chicken

Preparation Time: 15 minutes
Cooking Time: 40 minutes
Servings: 8

Ingredients:

- 1 (3½-pound) whole chicken, cut into 8 pieces
- Salt and ground black pepper, as required
- 2 cups buttermilk
- 2 cups all-purpose flour
- 1 tablespoon ground mustard
- 1 tablespoon garlic powder
- 1 tablespoon onion powder
- 1 tablespoon paprika

Preparation:

1. Rub the chicken pieces with salt and black pepper.
2. In a large bowl, add the chicken pieces and buttermilk and refrigerate to marinate for at least 1 hour.
3. Meanwhile, in a large bowl, place the flour, mustard, spices, salt and black pepper and mix well.
4. Remove the chicken pieces from bowl and drip off the excess buttermilk.
5. Coat the chicken pieces with the flour mixture, shaking any excess off.
6. Press "Power Button" of Ninja Foodi Digital Air Fry Oven and turn the dial to select "Air Fry" mode.
7. Press "Time Button" and again turn the dial to set the cooking time to 20 minutes.
8. Now push "Temp Button" and rotate the dial to set the temperature at 390 degrees F.
9. Press "Start/Pause" button to start.
10. When the unit beeps to show that it is preheated, open the lid and grease air fry basket.
11. Arrange half of the chicken pieces into air fry basket and insert in the oven
12. Repeat with the remaining chicken pieces.
13. When the cooking time is completed, open the lid and serve immediately.

Serving Suggestions: Serve alongside the French fries.

Variation Tip: Adjust the ratio of spices according to your taste.

Nutritional Information per Serving:

Calories: 518 | **Fat:** 8.5g|**Sat Fat:** 2.4g|**Carbohydrates:** 33.4g|**Fiber:** 1.8|**Sugar:** 4.3g|**Protein:** 72.6g

Parmesan Chicken Tenders

Preparation Time: 15 minutes
Cooking Time: 15 minutes
Servings: 4

Ingredients:

- ½ cup flour
- Salt and ground black pepper, as required
- 2 eggs, beaten
- ¾ cup panko breadcrumbs
- ¾ cup Parmesan cheese, grated finely
- 1 teaspoon Italian seasoning
- 8 chicken tenders

Preparation:

1. In a shallow dish, mix together the flour, salt and black pepper.
2. In a second shallow dish, place the beaten eggs.
3. In a third shallow dish, mix together the breadcrumbs, parmesan cheese and Italian seasoning.
4. Coat the chicken tenders with flour mixture, then dip into the beaten eggs and finally coat with breadcrumb mixture.
5. Arrange the tenders onto a greased sheet pan in a single layer.
6. Press "Power Button" of Ninja Foodi Digital Air Fry Oven and turn the dial to select "Air Fry" mode.
7. Press "Time Button" and again turn the dial to set the cooking time to 15 minutes.
8. Now push "Temp Button" and rotate the dial to set the temperature at 360 degrees F.
9. Press "Start/Pause" button to start.
10. When the unit beeps to show that it is preheated, open the lid and insert the sheet pan in oven.
11. When the cooking time is completed, open the lid and serve hot.

Serving Suggestions: Serve with blue cheese dip.

Variation Tip: Use dry breadcrumbs.

Nutritional Information per Serving:

Calories: 435 | **Fat:** 16.1g|**Sat Fat:** 5.4g|**Carbohydrates:** 15.3g|**Fiber:** 0g|**Sugar:** 0.5g|**Protein:** 0.4g

Lemony Chicken Thighs

Preparation Time: 15 minutes
Cooking Time: 20 minutes
Servings: 6

Ingredients:

- 6 (6-ounce) chicken thighs
- 2 tablespoons olive oil
- 2 tablespoons fresh lemon juice
- 1 tablespoon Italian seasoning
- Salt and ground black pepper, as required
- 1 lemon, sliced thinly

Preparation:

1. In a large bowl, add all the ingredients except for lemon slices and toss to coat well.
2. Refrigerate to marinate for 30 minutes to overnight.
3. Remove the chicken thighs from bowl and let any excess marinade drip off.
4. Press "Power Button" of Ninja Foodi Digital Air Fry Oven and turn the dial to select "Air Fry" mode.
5. Press "Time Button" and again turn the dial to set the cooking time to 20 minutes.
6. Now push "Temp Button" and rotate the dial to set the temperature at 350 degrees F.
7. Press "Start/Pause" button to start.
8. When the unit beeps to show that it is preheated, open the lid.
9. Arrange the chicken thighs into the greased air fry basket and insert the in oven.
10. Flip the chicken thighs once halfway through.
11. When the cooking time is completed, open the lid and serve hot alongside the lemon slices.

Serving Suggestions: Serve with your favorite salad.

Variation Tip: Make sure to use freshly squeezed lemon juice.

Nutritional Information per Serving:

Calories: 372 | **Fat:** 18g|**Sat Fat:** 4.3g|**Carbohydrates:** 0.6g|**Fiber:** 0.1g|**Sugar:** 0.4g|**Protein:** 49.3g

Herbed Chicken Thighs

Preparation Time: 10 minutes
Cooking Time: 20 minutes
Servings: 4

Ingredients:

- ½ tablespoon fresh rosemary, minced
- ½ tablespoon fresh thyme, minced
- Salt and ground black pepper, as required
- 4 (5-ounce) chicken thighs
- 2 tablespoons olive oil

Preparation:

1. In a large bowl, add the herbs, salt and black pepper and mix well.
2. Coat the chicken thighs with oil and then, rub with herb mixture.
3. Arrange the chicken thighs onto the greased sheet pan.
4. Press "Power Button" of Ninja Foodi Digital Air Fry Oven and turn the dial to select "Air Fry" mode.
5. Press "Time Button" and again turn the dial to set the cooking time to 20 minutes.
6. Now push "Temp Button" and rotate the dial to set the temperature at 400 degrees F.
7. Press "Start/Pause" button to start.
8. When the unit beeps to show that it is preheated, open the lid and insert the sheet pan in oven.
9. Flip the chicken thighs once halfway through.
10. When the cooking time is completed, open the lid and serve hot.

Serving Suggestions: Serve with couscous salad.

Variation Tip: Cook the chicken thighs until it reaches an internal temperature of 165° F.

Nutritional Information per Serving:

Calories: 332 | **Fat:** 17.6g|**Sat Fat:** 2.9g|**Carbohydrates:** 0.5g|**Fiber:** 0.3g|**Sugar:** 0g|**Protein:** 41.1g

Parmesan Crusted Chicken Breasts

Preparation Time: 15 minutes
Cooking Time: 15 minutes
Servings: 4

Ingredients:

- 2 large chicken breasts
- 1 cup mayonnaise
- 1 cup Parmesan cheese, shredded
- 1 cup panko breadcrumbs

Preparation:

1. Cut each chicken breast in half and then with a meat mallet pound each into even thickness.
2. Spread the mayonnaise on both sides of each chicken piece evenly.
3. In a shallow bowl, mix together the Parmesan and breadcrumbs.
4. Coat the chicken piece Parmesan mixture evenly.
5. Press "Power Button" of Ninja Foodi Digital Air Fry Oven and turn the dial to select "Air Fry" mode.
6. Press "Time Button" and again turn the dial to set the cooking time to 15 minutes.
7. Now push "Temp Button" and rotate the dial to set the temperature at 390 degrees F.
8. Press "Start/Pause" button to start.
9. When the unit beeps to show that it is preheated, open the lid.
10. Arrange the chicken pieces into the greased air fry basket and insert in the oven.
11. After 10 minutes of cooking, flip the chicken pieces once.
12. When the cooking time is completed, open the lid and serve hot.

Serving Suggestions: Serve with ranch dip.

Variation Tip: Use real mayonnaise.

Nutritional Information per Serving:

Calories: 625 | **Fat:** 35.4g|**Sat Fat:** 9.4g|**Carbohydrates:** 18.8g|**Fiber:** 0.1g|**Sugar:** 3.8g|**Protein:** 41.6g

Bacon-Wrapped Chicken Breasts

Preparation Time: 10 minutes
Cooking Time: 25 minutes
Servings: 2

Ingredients:

- 2 (5-6-ounce) boneless, skinless chicken breasts
- ½ teaspoon smoked paprika
- ½ teaspoon garlic powder
- Salt and ground black pepper, as required
- 4 thin bacon slices

Preparation:

1. With a meat mallet, pound each chicken breast into ¾-inch thickness.
2. In a bowl, mix together the paprika, garlic powder, salt and black pepper.
3. Rub the chicken breasts with spice mixture evenly.
4. Wrap each chicken breast with bacon strips.
5. Press "Power Button" of Ninja Foodi Digital Air Fry Oven and turn the dial to select "Air Fry" mode.
6. Press "Time Button" and again turn the dial to set the cooking time to 35 minutes.
7. Now push "Temp Button" and rotate the dial to set the temperature at 400 degrees F.
8. Press "Start/Pause" button to start.
9. When the unit beeps to show that it is preheated, open the lid.
10. Arrange the chicken pieces into the greased air fry basket and insert in the oven.
11. When the cooking time is completed, open the lid and serve hot.

Serving Suggestions: Serve with fresh baby greens.

Variation Tip: Secure the wrapping of bacon with toothpicks.

Nutritional Information per Serving:

Calories: 293 | **Fat:** 17.4g|**Sat Fat:** 5.4g|**Carbohydrates:** 0.8g|**Fiber:** 0.1g|**Sugar:** 0.1g|**Protein:** 31.3g

Spiced Chicken Breasts

Preparation Time: 10 minutes
Cooking Time: 35 minutes
Servings: 4

Ingredients:

- 1½ tablespoons smoked paprika
- 1 teaspoon ground cumin
- Salt and ground black pepper, as required
- 2 (12-ounce) chicken breasts
- 1 tablespoon olive oil

Preparation:

1. In a small bowl, mix together the paprika, cumin, salt and black pepper.
2. Coat the chicken breasts with oil evenly and then season with the spice mixture generously.
3. Press "Power Button" of Ninja Foodi Digital Air Fry Oven and turn the dial to select "Air Fry" mode.
4. Press "Time Button" and again turn the dial to set the cooking time to 35 minutes.
5. Now push "Temp Button" and rotate the dial to set the temperature at 375 degrees F.
6. Press "Start/Pause" button to start.
7. When the unit beeps to show that it is preheated, open the lid.
8. Arrange the peanuts into the air fry basket and insert in the oven.
9. When the cooking time is completed, open the lid and place the chicken breasts onto a cutting board for about 5 minutes.
10. Cut each breast in 2 equal-sized pieces and serve.

Serving Suggestions: Serve with sautéed kale.

Variation Tip: Fat of chicken breasts should always be white or deep yellow and never pale or gray.

Nutritional Information per Serving:

Calories: 363 | **Fat:** 16.6g|**Sat Fat:** 4g|**Carbohydrates:** 1.7g|**Fiber:** 1g|**Sugar:** 0.3g|**Protein:** 49.7g

Spiced Turkey Breast

Preparation Time: 10 minutes
Cooking Time: 45 minutes
Servings: 8

Ingredients:

- 2 tablespoons fresh rosemary, chopped
- 1 teaspoon ground cumin
- 1 teaspoon ground cinnamon
- 1 teaspoon smoked paprika
- 1 teaspoon cayenne pepper
- Salt and ground black pepper, as required
- 1 (3-pound) turkey breast

Preparation:

1. In a bowl, mix together the rosemary, spices, salt and black pepper.
2. Rub the turkey breast with rosemary mixture evenly.
3. With kitchen twines, tie the turkey breast to keep it compact.
4. Press "Power Button" of Ninja Foodi Digital Air Fry Oven and turn the dial to select "Air Fry" mode.
5. Press "Time Button" and again turn the dial to set the cooking time to 45 minutes.
6. Now push "Temp Button" and rotate the dial to set the temperature at 360 degrees F.
7. Press "Start/Pause" button to start.
8. When the unit beeps to show that it is preheated, open the lid.
9. Arrange the turkey breast into the greased air fry basket and insert in oven.
10. When the cooking time is completed, open the lid and place the turkey breast onto a platter for about 5-10 minutes before slicing.
11. With a sharp knife, cut the turkey breast into desired sized slices and serve.

Serving Suggestions: Serve alongside the cranberry sauce.

Variation Tip: Season the turkey breast generously.

Nutritional Information per Serving:

Calories: 190 | **Fat:** 0.9g|**Sat Fat:** 0.1g|**Carbohydrates:** 0.9g|**Fiber:** 0.5g|**Sugar:** 6g|**Protein:** 29.5g

Buttered Turkey Breast

Preparation Time: 15 minutes
Cooking Time: 1¼ hours
Servings: 10

Ingredients:

- ¼ cup butter
- 5 carrots, peeled and cut into chunks
- 1 (6-pound) boneless turkey breast
- Salt and ground black pepper, as required
- 1 cup chicken broth

Preparation:

1. In a pan, heat the oil over medium heat and the carrots for about 4-5 minutes.
2. Add the turkey breast and cook for about 10 minutes or until golden brown from both sides.
3. Remove from the heat and stir in salt, black pepper and broth.
4. Transfer the mixture into a baking dish.
5. Press "Power Button" of Ninja Foodi Digital Air Fry Oven and turn the dial to select "Air Bake" mode.
6. Press "Time Button" and again turn the dial to set the cooking time to 60 minutes.
7. Now push "Temp Button" and rotate the dial to set the temperature at 375 degrees F.
8. Press "Start/Pause" button to start.
9. When the unit beeps to show that it is preheated, open the lid.
10. Arrange the baking dish over the wire rack and insert in the oven.
11. When the cooking time is completed, open the lid and with tongs, place the turkey onto a cutting board for about 5 minutes before slicing.
12. Cut into desired-sized slices and serve alongside carrots.

Serving Suggestions: Serve with fresh salad.

Variation Tip: You can also cook fennel and parsnip alongside the carrot in this recipe.

Nutritional Information per Serving:

Calories: 322 | **Fat:** 6g|**Sat Fat:** 3g|**Carbohydrates:** 3.1g|**Fiber:** 0.8g|**Sugar:** 1.6g|**Protein:** 6.2g

Simple Turkey Wings

Preparation Time: 10 minutes
Cooking Time: 26 minutes
Servings: 4

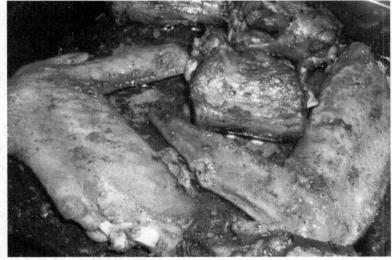

Ingredients:

- 2 pounds turkey wings
- 4 tablespoons chicken rub
- 3 tablespoons olive oil

Preparation:

1. In a large bowl, add the turkey wings, chicken rub and olive oil and toss to coat well.
2. Press "Power Button" of Ninja Foodi Digital Air Fry Oven and turn the dial to select "Air Fry" mode.
3. Press "Time Button" and again turn the dial to set the cooking time to 26 minutes.
4. Now push "Temp Button" and rotate the dial to set the temperature at 380 degrees F.
5. Press "Start/Pause" button to start.
6. When the unit beeps to show that it is preheated, open the lid.
7. Arrange the turkey wings into the greased air fry basket and insert in the oven.
8. Flip the turkey wings once halfway through.
9. When the cooking time is completed, open the lid and serve hot.

Serving Suggestions: Serve alongside the yogurt suace.

Variation Tip: You can use seasoning of your choice.

Nutritional Information per Serving:

Calories: 558 | **Fat:** 38.9g|**Sat Fat:** 1.5g|**Carbohydrates:** 3g|**Fiber:** 0g|**Sugar:** 0g|**Protein:** 46.6g

Herbed Turkey Legs

Preparation Time: 15 minutes
Cooking Time: 30 minutes
Servings: 2

Ingredients:

- 1 tablespoon butter, melted
- 2 garlic cloves, minced
- ¼ teaspoon dried rosemary
- ¼ teaspoon dried thyme
- ¼ teaspoon dried oregano
- Salt and ground black pepper, as required
- 2 turkey legs

Preparation:

1. In a large bowl, mix together the butter, garlic, herbs, salt, and black pepper.
2. Add the turkey legs and coat with mixture generously.
3. Press "Power Button" of Ninja Foodi Digital Air Fry Oven and turn the dial to select "Air Fry" mode.
4. Press "Time Button" and again turn the dial to set the cooking time to 27 minutes.
5. Now push "Temp Button" and rotate the dial to set the temperature at 350 degrees F.
6. Press "Start/Pause" button to start.
7. When the unit beeps to show that it is preheated, open the lid.
8. Arrange the turkey wings into the greased air fry basket and insert in the oven.
9. When the cooking time is completed, open the lid and serve hot.

Serving Suggestions: Serve with cabbage slaw.

Variation Tip: Use unsalted butter.

Nutritional Information per Serving:

Calories: 592 | **Fat:** 22g|**Sat Fat:** 8.7g|**Carbohydrates:** 1.3g|**Fiber:** 0.3g|**Sugar:** 0g|**Protein:** 91.6g

Feta Turkey Burgers

Preparation Time: 10 minutes
Cooking Time: 15 minutes
Servings: 2

Ingredients:

- 8 ounces ground turkey breast
- 1½ tablespoons extra-virgin olive oil
- 2 garlic cloves, grated
- 2 teaspoons fresh oregano, chopped
- ½ teaspoon red pepper flakes, crushed
- Salt, as required
- ¼ cup feta cheese, crumbled

Preparation:

1. In a large bowl, add all the ingredients except for cheese and mix until well combined.
2. Make 2 (½-inch-thick) patties from the mixture.
3. Press "Power Button" of Ninja Foodi Digital Air Fry Oven and turn the dial to select "Air Fry" mode.
4. Press "Time Button" and again turn the dial to set the cooking time to 15 minutes.
5. Now push "Temp Button" and rotate the dial to set the temperature at 360 degrees F.
6. Press "Start/Pause" button to start.
7. When the unit beeps to show that it is preheated, open the lid.
8. Arrange the patties into the greased air fry basket and insert in the oven.
9. Flip the turkey burgers once halfway through.
10. When the cooking time is completed, open the lid and serve hot with the topping of feta.

Serving Suggestions: Serve with fresh greens.

Variation Tip: Try adding some dry breadcrumbs to the turkey mixture before you shape the patties.

Nutritional Information per Serving:

Calories: 364 | **Fat:** 23.1g|**Sat Fat:** 6.7g|**Carbohydrates:** 3g|**Fiber:** 0.8g|**Sugar:** 0.9g|**Protein:** 35.6g

Molasses Glazed Duck Breast

Preparation Time: 15 minutes
Cooking Time: 44 minutes
Servings: 3

Ingredients:

- 2 cups fresh pomegranate juice
- 2 tablespoons fresh lemon juice
- 3 tablespoons brown sugar
- 1 pound boneless duck breast
- Salt and ground black pepper, as required

Preparation:

1. For pomegranate molasses: in a medium saucepan, add the pomegranate juice, lemon and brown sugar over medium heat and bring to a boil.
2. Reduce the heat to low and simmer for about 25 minutes until the mixture is thick.
3. Remove from the hat and set aside to cool slightly
4. Meanwhile, with a knife, make the slit on the duck breast.
5. Season the duck breast with salt and black pepper generously.
6. Press "Power Button" of Ninja Foodi Digital Air Fry Oven and turn the dial to select "Air Fry" mode.
7. Press "Time Button" and again turn the dial to set the cooking time to 14 minutes.
8. Now push "Temp Button" and rotate the dial to set the temperature at 400 degrees F.
9. Press "Start/Pause" button to start.
10. When the unit beeps to show that it is preheated, open the lid.
11. Arrange the duck breast into the greased air fry basket, skin side up and insert in the oven.
12. After 6 minutes of cooking, flip the duck breast.
13. When the cooking time is completed, open the lid and place the duck breast onto a platter for about 5 minutes before slicing.
14. With a sharp knife, cut the duck breast into desired sized slices and transfer onto a platter.
15. Drizzle with warm molasses and serve.

Serving Suggestions: Serve alongside the garlicky sweet potatoes.

Variation Tip: You can also use store-bought pomegranate molasses.

Nutritional Information per Serving:

Calories: 332 | **Fat:** 6.1g|**Sat Fat:** 0.1g|**Carbohydrates:** 337g|**Fiber:** 0g|**Sugar:** 31.6g|**Protein:** 34g

Red Meat Recipes

Buttered Strip Steak

Preparation Time: 10 minutes
Cooking Time: 8 minutes
Servings: 4

Ingredients:

- 2 (14-ounce) New York strip steaks
- 2 tablespoons butter, melted
- Salt and ground black pepper, as required

Preparation:

1. Brush each steak with the melted butter evenly and then season with salt and black pepper.
2. Press "Power Button" of Ninja Foodi Digital Air Fry Oven and turn the dial to select the "Air Broil" mode.
3. Press "Time Button" and again turn the dial to set the cooking time to 15 minutes.
4. Press "Start/Pause" button to start.
5. When the unit beeps to show that it is preheated, open the lid.
6. Place the steaks over the wire rack and insert in oven.
7. When cooking time is completed, open the lid and place the steaks onto a cutting board for about 5 minutes before slicing.
8. Cut each steak into 2 portions and serve.

Serving Suggestions: Serve alongside the spiced potatoes.

Variation Tip: Tru to use freshly ground black pepper.

Nutritional Information per Serving:

Calories: 296 | **Fat:** 12.7g|**Sat Fat:** 6.6g|**Carbohydrates:** 0g|**Fiber:** 0g|**Sugar:** 0g|**Protein:** 44.5g

Crispy Sirloin Steaks

Preparation Time: 10 minutes
Cooking Time: 14 minutes
Servings: 2

Ingredients:

- ½ cup flour
- Salt and ground black pepper, as required
- 2 eggs
- ¾ cup breadcrumbs
- 3 (6-ounce) sirloin steaks, pounded

Preparation:

1. In a shallow bowl, place the flour, salt and black pepper and mix well.
2. In a second shallow bowl, beat the eggs.
3. In a third shallow bowl, place the breadcrumbs.
4. Coat the steak with flour, then dip into eggs, and finally coat with the panko mixture.
5. Press "Power Button" of Ninja Foodi Digital Air Fry Oven and turn the dial to select "Air Fry" mode.
6. Press "Time Button" and again turn the dial to set the cooking time to 14 minutes.
7. Now push "Temp Button" and rotate the dial to set the temperature at 360 degrees F.
8. Press "Start/Pause" button to start.
9. When the unit beeps to show that it is preheated, open the lid.
10. Arrange the steaks into the greased air fry basket and insert in the oven.
11. When the cooking time is completed, open the lid and serve hot.

Serving Suggestions: Serve with your favorite dipping sauce.

Variation Tip: Feel free to use breadcrumbs of your choice.

Nutritional Information per Serving:

Calories: 540 | **Fat:** 15.2g|**Sat Fat:** 5.3g|**Carbohydrates:** 35.6g|**Fiber:** 1.8g|**Sugar:** 2g|**Protein:** 61g

Glazed Beef Short Ribs

Preparation Time: 15 minutes
Cooking Time: 8 minutes
Servings: 4

Ingredients:

- 2 pounds bone-in beef short ribs
- 3 tablespoons scallions, chopped
- ½ tablespoon fresh ginger, finely grated
- ½ cup low-sodium soy sauce
- ¼ cup balsamic vinegar
- ½ tablespoon Sriracha
- 1 tablespoon sugar
- ½ teaspoon ground black pepper

Preparation:

1. In a resealable bag, place all the ingredients.
2. Seal the bag and shake to coat well.
3. Refrigerate overnight.
4. Press "Power Button" of Ninja Foodi Digital Air Fry Oven and turn the dial to select "Air Fry" mode.
5. Press "Time Button" and again turn the dial to set the cooking time to 8 minutes.
6. Now push "Temp Button" and rotate the dial to set the temperature at 380 degrees F.
7. Press "Start/Pause" button to start.
8. When the unit beeps to show that it is preheated, open the lid.
9. Place the ribs into the greased air fry basket and insert in the oven.
10. Flip the ribs once halfway through.
11. When the cooking time is completed, open the lid and serve hot.

Serving Suggestions: Serve with cucumber salad.

Variation Tip: Brown sugar can also be used in this recipe.

Nutritional Information per Serving:

Calories: 496 | **Fat:** 20.5g|**Sat Fat:** 7.8g|**Carbohydrates:** 6.5g|**Fiber:** 0.3g|**Sugar:** 5.2g|**Protein:** 67.7g

Balsamic Beef Top Roast

Preparation Time: 10 minutes
Cooking Time: 45 minutes
Servings: 10

Ingredients:

- 1 tablespoon butter, melted
- 1 tablespoon balsamic vinegar
- ½ teaspoon ground cumin
- ½ teaspoon smoked paprika
- ½ teaspoon red pepper flakes, crushed
- Salt and ground black pepper, as required
- 3 pounds beef top roast

Preparation:

1. In a bowl, add butter, vinegar, spices, salt and black pepper and mix well.
2. Coat the roast with spice mixture generously.
3. With kitchen twines, tie the roast to keep it compact.
4. Arrange the roast onto the greased sheet pan.
5. Press "Power Button" of Ninja Foodi Digital Air Fry Oven and turn the dial to select "Air Fry" mode.
6. Press "Time Button" and again turn the dial to set the cooking time to 45 minutes.
7. Now push "Temp Button" and rotate the dial to set the temperature at 360 degrees F.
8. Press "Start/Pause" button to start.
9. When the unit beeps to show that it is preheated, open the lid and insert the sheet pan in the oven.
10. When the cooking time is completed, open the lid and place the roast onto a cutting board for about 10 minutes before slicing.
11. With a sharp knife, cut the roast into desired sized slices and serve.

Serving Suggestions: Serve alongside the buttered green beans.

Variation Tip: Use unsalted butter.

Nutritional Information per Serving:

Calories: 305 | **Fat:** 17.1g|**Sat Fat:** 6.1g|**Carbohydrates:** 0.1g|**Fiber:** 0.1g|**Sugar:** 0g|**Protein:** 35.1g

Simple Pork Chops

Preparation Time: 10 minutes
Cooking Time: 18 minutes
Servings: 2

Ingredients:

- 2 (6-ounce) (½-inch thick) pork chops
- Salt and ground black pepper, as required

Preparation:

1. Season the pork chops with salt and black pepper evenly.
2. Arrange the pork chops onto a greased baking pan.
3. Press "Power Button" of Ninja Foodi Digital Air Fry Oven and turn the dial to select the "Air Broil" mode.
4. Press "Time Button" and again turn the dial to set the cooking time to 18 minutes.
5. Press "Start/Pause" button to start.
6. When the unit beeps to show that it is preheated, open the lid and insert the baking pan in oven.
7. After 12 minutes of cooking, flip the chops once.
8. When cooking time is completed, open the lid and serve hot.

Serving Suggestions: Serve alongside the mashed potato.

Variation Tip: Season the chops generously.

Nutritional Information per Serving:

Calories: 544 | **Fat:** 42.3g|**Sat Fat:** 15.8g|**Carbohydrates:** 0g|**Fiber:** 0g|**Sugar:** 0g|**Protein:** 38.2g

Citrus Pork Chops

Preparation Time: 15 minutes
Cooking Time: 15 minutes
Servings: 6

Ingredients:

- ½ cup olive oil
- 1 teaspoon fresh orange zest, grated
- 3 tablespoons fresh orange juice
- 1 teaspoon fresh lime zest, grated
- 3 tablespoons fresh lime juice
- 8 garlic cloves, minced
- 1 cup fresh cilantro, chopped finely
- ¼ cup fresh mint leaves, chopped finely
- 1 teaspoon dried oregano, crushed
- 1 teaspoon ground cumin
- Salt and ground black pepper, as required
- 6 thick-cut pork chops

Preparation:

1. In a bowl, place the oil, orange zest, orange juice, lime zest, lime juice, garlic, fresh herbs, oregano, cumin, salt and black pepper and beat until well combined.
2. In a small bowl, reserve ¼ cup of the marinade.
3. In a large zip lock bag, place the remaining marinade and pork chops.
4. Seal the bag and shake to coat well.
5. Refrigerate to marinate overnight.
6. Remove the pork chops from the bag and shake off to remove the excess marinade.
7. Press "Power Button" of Ninja Foodi Digital Air Fry Oven and turn the dial to select the "Air Broil" mode.
8. Press "Time Button" and again turn the dial to set the cooking time to 15 minutes.
9. Press "Start/Pause" button to start.
10. When the unit beeps to show that it is preheated, open the lid.
11. Place the pork chops over the wire rack and insert in oven.
12. After 8 minutes of cooking, flip the chops once.
13. When the cooking time is completed, open the lid and serve hot.

Serving Suggestions: Serve with steamed broccoli.

Variation Tip: Use fresh orange juice and zest.

Nutritional Information per Serving:

Calories: 700 | **Fat:** 59.3g|**Sat Fat:** 18.3g|**Carbohydrates:** 2.1g|**Fiber:** 0.4g|**Sugar:** 0.3g|**Protein:** 38.7g

BBQ Pork Chops

Preparation Time: 10 minutes
Cooking Time: 16 minutes
Servings: 6

Ingredients:

- 6 (8-ounce) pork loin chops
- Salt and ground black pepper, as required
- ½ cup BBQ sauce

Preparation:

1. With a meat tenderizer, tenderize the chops completely.
2. Sprinkle the chops with a little salt and black pepper.
3. In a large bowl, add the BBQ sauce and chops and mix well.
4. Refrigerate, covered for about 6-8 hours.
5. Press "Power Button" of Ninja Foodi Digital Air Fry Oven and turn the dial to select "Air Fry" mode.
6. Press "Time Button" and again turn the dial to set the cooking time to 16 minutes.
7. Now push "Temp Button" and rotate the dial to set the temperature at 355 degrees F.
8. Press "Start/Pause" button to start.
9. When the unit beeps to show that it is preheated, open the lid.
10. Arrange the pork chops into the greased air fry basket and insert in the oven.
11. Flip the chops once halfway through.
12. When the cooking time is completed, open the lid and serve hot.

Serving Suggestions: Serve with roasted veggies.

Variation Tip: Make sure to use good quality BBQ sauce.

Nutritional Information per Serving:

Calories: 757 | **Fat:** 56.4g|**Sat Fat:** 21.1g|**Carbohydrates:** 7.6g|**Fiber:** 0.1g|**Sugar:** 5.4g|**Protein:** 51g

Spiced Pork Shoulder

Preparation Time: 15 minutes
Cooking Time: 55 minutes
Servings: 6

Ingredients:

* 1 teaspoon ground cumin
* 1 teaspoon cayenne pepper
* 1 teaspoon garlic powder
* Salt and ground black pepper, as required
* 2 pounds skin-on pork shoulder

Preparation:

1. In a small bowl, mix together the spices, salt and black pepper.
2. Arrange the pork shoulder onto a cutting board, skin-side down.
3. Season the inner side of pork shoulder with salt and black pepper.
4. With kitchen twines, tie the pork shoulder into a long round cylinder shape.
5. Season the outer side of pork shoulder with spice mixture.
6. Press "Power Button" of Ninja Foodi Digital Air Fry Oven and turn the dial to select "Air Roast" mode.
7. Press "Time Button" and again turn the dial to set the cooking time to 55 minutes.
8. Now push "Temp Button" and rotate the dial to set the temperature at 350 degrees F.
9. Press "Start/Pause" button to start.
10. When the unit beeps to show that it is preheated, open the lid.
11. Arrange the pork shoulder into the greased air fry basket and insert in the oven.
12. When cooking time is complete, open the lid and place the pork shoulder onto a platter for about 10 minutes before slicing.
13. With a sharp knife, cut the pork shoulder into desired sized slices and serve.

Serving Suggestions: Serve with steamed veggies.

Variation Tip: Make sure to trim the fat.

Nutritional Information per Serving:

Calories: 445 | **Fat:** 32.5g|**Sat Fat:** 11.9g|**Carbohydrates:** 0.7g|**Fiber:** 0.2g|**Sugar:** 0.2g|**Protein:** 35.4g

Herbed Leg of Lamb

Preparation Time: 10 minutes
Cooking Time: 1¼ hours
Servings: 6

Ingredients:

- 2¼ pounds boneless leg of lamb
- 2 tablespoons olive oil
- Salt and ground black pepper, as required
- 2 fresh rosemary sprigs
- 2 fresh thyme sprigs

Preparation:

1. Coat the leg of lamb with oil and sprinkle with salt and black pepper.
2. Wrap the leg of lamb with herb sprigs.
3. Press "Power Button" of Ninja Foodi Digital Air Fry Oven and turn the dial to select "Air Fry" mode.
4. Press "Time Button" and again turn the dial to set the cooking time to 75 minutes.
5. Now push "Temp Button" and rotate the dial to set the temperature at 300 degrees F.
6. Press "Start/Pause" button to start.
7. When the unit beeps to show that it is preheated, open the lid.
8. Arrange the leg of lamb into the greased air fry basket and insert in the oven.
9. Immediately set the temperature at 355 degrees F.
10. When the cooking time is completed, open the lid and place the leg of lamb onto a cutting board for about 10 minutes.
11. Cut the leg of lamb into desired-sized pieces and serve.

Serving Suggestions: Serve alongside the roasted Brussels sprout.

Variation Tip: Always slice the meat against the grain.

Nutritional Information per Serving:

Calories: 360 | **Fat:** 17.3g|**Sat Fat:** 5.2g|**Carbohydrates:** 0.7g|**Fiber:** 0.5g|**Sugar:** 0g|**Protein:** 47.8g

Lamb Chops with Carrots

Preparation Time: 15 minutes
Cooking Time: 10 minutes
Servings: 4

Ingredients:

- 2 tablespoons fresh rosemary, minced
- 2 tablespoons fresh mint leaves, minced
- 1 garlic clove, minced
- 3 tablespoons olive oil
- Salt and ground black pepper, as required
- 4 (6-ounces) lamb chops
- 2 large carrots, peeled and cubed

Preparation:

1. In a large bowl, mix together the herbs, garlic, oil, salt, and black pepper.
2. Add the chops and generously coat with mixture.
3. Refrigerate to marinate for about 3 hours.
4. In a large pan of water, soak the carrots for about 15 minutes.
5. Drain the carrots completely.
6. Press "Power Button" of Ninja Foodi Digital Air Fry Oven and turn the dial to select "Air Fry" mode.
7. Press "Time Button" and again turn the dial to set the cooking time to 10 minutes.
8. Now push "Temp Button" and rotate the dial to set the temperature at 390 degrees F.
9. Press "Start/Pause" button to start.
10. When the unit beeps to show that it is preheated, open the lid.
11. Arrange chops into the greased air fry basket in a single layer and insert in the oven.
12. After 2 minutes of cooking, arrange carrots into the air fry basket and top with the chops in a single layer.
13. Insert the basket in oven.
14. When the cooking time is completed, open the lid and transfer the chops and carrots onto serving plates.
15. Serve hot.

Serving Suggestions: Serve with fresh greens.

Variation Tip: You can use herbs of your choice.

Nutritional Information per Serving:

Calories: 429 | **Fat:** 23.2g|**Sat Fat:** 6.1g|**Carbohydrates:** 5.1g|**Fiber:** 1.8g|**Sugar:** 1.8g|**Protein:** 48.3g

Mustard Lamb Loin Chops

Preparation Time: 10 minutes
Cooking Time: 15 minutes
Servings: 2

Ingredients:

- 1 tablespoon Dijon mustard
- ½ tablespoon white wine vinegar
- 1 teaspoon olive oil
- ½ teaspoon dried tarragon
- Salt and ground black pepper, as required
- 4 (4-ounce) lamb loin chops

Preparation:

1. In a large bowl, mix together the mustard, vinegar, oil, tarragon, salt, and black pepper.
2. Add the chops and coat with the mixture generously.
3. Arrange the chops onto the greased sheet pan.
4. Press "Power Button" of Ninja Foodi Digital Air Fry Oven and turn the dial to select "Air Bake" mode.
5. Press "Time Button" and again turn the dial to set the cooking time to 15 minutes.
6. Now push "Temp Button" and rotate the dial to set the temperature at 390 degrees F.
7. Press "Start/Pause" button to start.
8. When the unit beeps to show that it is preheated, open the lid and insert the sheet pan in the oven.
9. When the cooking time is completed, open the lid and serve hot.

Serving Suggestions: Serve alongside the feta spinach.

Variation Tip: Remember to bring the chops to room temperature.

Nutritional Information per Serving:

Calories: 44 | **Fat:** 19.3g|**Sat Fat:** 6.3g|**Carbohydrates:** 0.5g|**Fiber:** 0.3g|**Sugar:** 0.1g|**Protein:** 64.1g

Herbed Lamb Loin Chops

Preparation Time: 10 minutes
Cooking Time: 12 minutes
Servings: 2

Ingredients:

- 4 (4-ounce) (½-inch thick) lamb loin chops
- 1 teaspoon fresh thyme, minced
- 1 teaspoon fresh rosemary, minced
- 1 teaspoon fresh oregano, minced
- 2 garlic cloves, crushed
- Salt and ground black pepper, as required

Preparation:

1. In a large bowl, place all ingredients and mix well.
2. Refrigerate to marinate overnight.
3. Arrange the chops onto the greased sheet pan.
4. Press "Power Button" of Ninja Foodi Digital Air Fry Oven and turn the dial to select "Air Bake" mode.
5. Press "Time Button" and again turn the dial to set the cooking time to 12 minutes.
6. Now push "Temp Button" and rotate the dial to set the temperature at 400 degrees F.
7. Press "Start/Pause" button to start.
8. When the unit beeps to show that it is preheated, open the lid and insert the sheet pan in the oven.
9. Flip the chops once halfway through.
10. When the cooking time is completed, open the lid and serve hot. s

Serving Suggestions: Serve with steamed cauliflower.

Variation Tip: Season the chops nicely.

Nutritional Information per Serving:

Calories: 432 | **Fat:** 16.9g|**Sat Fat:** 6g|**Carbohydrates:** 2.2g|**Fiber:** 0.8g|**Sugar:** 0.1g|**Protein:** 64g

Dessert Recipes

Walnut Brownies

Preparation Time: 15 minutes
Cooking Time: 22 minutes
Servings: 4
Ingredients:

- ½ cup chocolate, roughly chopped
- 1/3 cup butter
- 5 tablespoons sugar
- 1 egg, beaten
- 1 teaspoon vanilla extract
- Pinch of salt
- 5 tablespoons self-rising flour
- ¼ cup walnuts, chopped

Preparation:

1. In a microwave-safe bowl, add the chocolate and butter. Microwave on high heat for about 2 minutes, stirring after every 30 seconds.
2. Remove from microwave and set aside to cool.
3. In another bowl, add the sugar, egg, vanilla extract, and salt and whisk until creamy and light.
4. Add the chocolate mixture and whisk until well combined.
5. Add the flour, and walnuts and mix until well combined.
6. Line a baking pan with a greased parchment paper.
7. Place mixture into the prepared pan and with the back of spatula, smooth the top surface.
8. Press "Power Button" of Ninja Foodi Digital Air Fry Oven and turn the dial to select "Air Fry" mode.
9. Press "Time Button" and again turn the dial to set the cooking time to 20 minutes.
10. Now push "Temp Button" and rotate the dial to set the temperature at 355 degrees F.
11. Press "Start/Pause" button to start.
12. When the unit beeps to show that it is preheated, open the lid.
13. Arrange the pan into the air fry basket and insert in the oven.
14. When cooking time is completed, open the lid and place the baking pan onto a wire rack to cool completely.
15. Cut into 4 equal-sized squares and serve.

Serving Suggestions: Serve with the dusting of powdered sugar.

Variation Tip: You can also use almond extract n the recipe.

Nutritional Information per Serving:
Calories: 407 | **Fat:** 27.4g|**Sat Fat:** 14.7g|**Carbohydrates:** 35.9g|**Fiber:** 1.5g|**Sugar:** 26.2g|**Protein:** 6g

Nutella Banana Pastries

Preparation Time: 15 minutes
Cooking Time: 12 minutes
Servings: 4

Ingredients:

- 1 puff pastry sheet
- ½ cup Nutella
- 2 bananas, peeled and sliced

Preparation:

1. Cut the pastry sheet into 4 equal-sized squares.
2. Spread the Nutella on each square of pastry evenly.
3. Divide the banana slices over Nutella.
4. Fold each square into a triangle and with wet fingers, slightly press the edges.
5. Then with a fork, press the edges firmly.
6. Press "Power Button" of Ninja Foodi Digital Air Fry Oven and turn the dial to select "Air Fry" mode.
7. Press "Time Button" and again turn the dial to set the cooking time to 12 minutes.
8. Now push "Temp Button" and rotate the dial to set the temperature at 375 degrees F.
9. Press "Start/Pause" button to start.
10. When the unit beeps to show that it is preheated, open the lid.
11. Arrange the pastries into the greased air fry basket and insert in the oven.
12. When cooking time is completed, open the lid and serve warm.

Serving Suggestions: Serve with the sprinkling of cinnamon.

Variation Tip: You can use the fruit of your choice.

Nutritional Information per Serving:

Calories: 221 | **Fat:** 10g|**Sat Fat:** 2.7g|**Carbohydrates:** 31.6g|**Fiber:** 2.6g|**Sugar:** 14.4g|**Protein:** 3.4g

Chocolate Soufflé

Preparation Time: 15 minutes
Cooking Time: 16 minutes
Servings: 2

Ingredients:

- 3 ounces semi-sweet chocolate, chopped
- ¼ cup butter
- 2 eggs, yolks and whites separated
- 3 tablespoons sugar
- ½ teaspoon pure vanilla extract
- 2 tablespoons all-purpose flour
- 1 teaspoon powdered sugar plus extra for dusting

Preparation:

1. In a microwave-safe bowl, place the butter and chocolate. Microwave on high heat for about 2 minutes or until melted completely, stirring after every 30 seconds.
2. Remove from the microwave and stir the mixture until smooth.
3. In another bowl, add the egg yolks and whisk well.
4. Add the sugar and vanilla extract and whisk well.
5. Add the chocolate mixture and mix until well combined.
6. Add the flour and mix well.
7. In a clean glass bowl, add the egg whites and whisk until soft peaks form.
8. Fold the whipped egg whites in 3 portions into the chocolate mixture.
9. Grease 2 ramekins and sprinkle each with a pinch of sugar.
10. Place mixture into the prepared ramekins and with the back of a spoon, smooth the top surface.
11. Press "Power Button" of Ninja Foodi Digital Air Fry Oven and turn the dial to select "Air Fry" mode.
12. Press "Time Button" and again turn the dial to set the cooking time to 14 minutes.
13. Now push "Temp Button" and rotate the dial to set the temperature at 330 degrees F.
14. Press "Start/Pause" button to start.
15. When the unit beeps to show that it is preheated, open the lid.
16. Arrange the ramekins into the air fry basket and insert in the oven.
17. When cooking time is completed, open the lid and place the ramekins onto a wire rack to cool slightly.
18. Sprinkle with the powdered sugar and serve warm.

Serving Suggestions: Serve with the garnishing of berries.

Variation Tip: Use high-quality chocolate.

Nutritional Information per Serving:

Calories: 591 | **Fat:** 87.3g|**Sat Fat:** 23g|**Carbohydrates:** 52.6g|**Fiber:** 0.2g|**Sugar:** 41.1g|**Protein:** 9.4g

Brownie Muffins

Preparation Time: 10 minutes
Cooking Time: 10 minutes
Servings: 12

Ingredients:

- 1 package Betty Crocker fudge brownie mix
- ¼ cup walnuts, chopped
- 1 egg
- 1/3 cup vegetable oil
- 2 teaspoons water

Preparation:

1. Grease 12 muffin molds. Set aside.
2. In a bowl, mix together all the ingredients.
3. Place the mixture into the prepared muffin molds.
4. Press "Power Button" of Ninja Foodi Digital Air Fry Oven and turn the dial to select "Air Fry" mode.
5. Press "Time Button" and again turn the dial to set the cooking time to 10 minutes.
6. Now push "Temp Button" and rotate the dial to set the temperature at 300 degrees F.
7. Press "Start/Pause" button to start.
8. When the unit beeps to show that it is preheated, open the lid.
9. Arrange the muffin molds into the air fry basket and insert in the oven.
10. When cooking time is completed, open the lid and place the muffin molds onto a wire rack to cool for about 10 minutes.
11. Carefully invert the muffins onto the wire rack to completely cool before serving.

Serving Suggestions: Serve with the topping of coconut.

Variation Tip: You can use oil of your choice.

Nutritional Information per Serving:

Calories: 168 | **Fat:** 8.9g|**Sat Fat:** 1.4g|**Carbohydrates:** 20.8g|**Fiber:** 1.1g|**Sugar:** 14g|**Protein:** 2g

Strawberry Cupcakes

Preparation Time: 20 minutes
Cooking Time: 8 minutes
Servings: 10

Ingredients:

For Cupcakes:

- ½ cup caster sugar
- 7 tablespoons butter
- 2 eggs
- ½ teaspoon vanilla essence
- 7/8 cup self-rising flour

For Frosting:

- 1 cup icing sugar
- 3½ tablespoons butter
- 1 tablespoon whipped cream
- ¼ cup fresh strawberries, pureed
- ½ teaspoon pink food color

Preparation:

1. In a bowl, add the butter and sugar and beat until fluffy and light.
2. Add the eggs, one at a time and beat until well combined.
3. Stir in the vanilla extract.
4. Gradually, add the flour, beating continuously until well combined.
5. Place the mixture into 10 silicone cups.
6. Press "Power Button" of Ninja Foodi Digital Air Fry Oven and turn the dial to select "Air Fry" mode.
7. Press "Time Button" and again turn the dial to set the cooking time to 8 minutes.
8. Now push "Temp Button" and rotate the dial to set the temperature at 340 degrees F.
9. Press "Start/Pause" button to start.
10. When the unit beeps to show that it is preheated, open the lid.
11. Arrange the silicone cups into the air fry basket and insert in the oven.
12. When cooking time is completed, open the lid and place the silicon cups onto a wire rack to cool for about 10 minutes.
13. Carefully invert the muffins onto the wire rack to completely cool before frosting.
14. For frosting: in a bowl, add the icing sugar and butter and whisk until fluffy and light.
15. Add the whipped cream, strawberry puree, and color. Mix until well combined.
16. Fill the pastry bag with frosting and decorate the cupcakes.

Serving Suggestions: Serve with the garnishing of fresh strawberries.

Variation Tip: Use room temperature eggs.

Nutritional Information per Serving:

Calories: 250 | **Fat:** 13.6g|**Sat Fat:** 8.2g|**Carbohydrates:** 30.7g|**Fiber:** 0.4g|**Sugar:** 22.1g|**Protein:** 2.4g

Carrot Mug Cake

Preparation Time: 10 minutes
Cooking Time: 20 minutes
Servings: 1

Ingredients:

- ¼ cup whole-wheat pastry flour
- 1 tablespoon coconut sugar
- ¼ teaspoon baking powder
- 1/8 teaspoon ground cinnamon
- 1/8 teaspoon ground ginger
- Pinch of ground cloves
- Pinch of ground allspice
- Pinch of salt
- 2 tablespoons plus 2 teaspoons unsweetened almond milk
- 2 tablespoons carrot, peeled and grated
- 2 tablespoons walnuts, chopped
- 1 tablespoon raisins
- 2 teaspoons applesauce

Preparation:

1. In a bowl, mix together the flour, sugar, baking powder, spices and salt.
2. Add the remaining ingredients and mix until well combined
3. Place the mixture into a lightly greased ramekin.
4. Press "Power Button" of Ninja Foodi Digital Air Fry Oven and turn the dial to select the "Air Bake" mode.
5. Press "Time Button" and again turn the dial to set the cooking time to 20 minutes.
6. Now push "Temp Button" and rotate the dial to set the temperature at 350 degrees F.
7. Press "Start/Pause" button to start.
8. When the unit beeps to show that it is preheated, open the lid.
9. Arrange the ramekin over the wire rack and insert in the oven.
10. When cooking time is completed, open the lid and place the ramekin onto a wire rack to cool slightly before serving.

Serving Suggestions: Serve with the topping of whipped cream.

Variation Tip: Applesauce can be replaced with honey.

Nutritional Information per Serving:

Calories: 301 | **Fat:** 10.1g|**Sat Fat:** 0.7g|**Carbohydrates:** 48.6g|**Fiber:** 3.2g|**Sugar:** 19.4g|**Protein:** 7.6g

Blueberry Cobbler

Preparation Time: 15 minutes
Cooking Time: 20 minutes
Servings: 6

Ingredients:

For Filling:

- 2½ cups fresh blueberries
- 1 teaspoon vanilla extract
- 1 teaspoon fresh lemon juice
- 1 cup sugar
- 1 teaspoon flour
- 1 tablespoon butter, melted

For Topping:

- 1¾ cups all-purpose flour
- 6 tablespoons sugar
- 4 teaspoons baking powder
- 1 cup milk
- 5 tablespoons butter

For Sprinkling:

- 2 teaspoons sugar
- ¼ teaspoon ground cinnamon

Preparation:

1. For filling: in a bowl, add all the ingredients and mix until well combined.
2. For topping: in another large bowl, mix together the flour, baking powder, and sugar.
3. Add the milk and butter and mix until a crumply mixture forms.
4. For sprinkling: in a small bowl mix together the sugar and cinnamon.
5. In the bottom of a greased pan, place the blueberries mixture and top with the flour mixture evenly.
6. Sprinkle the cinnamon sugar on top evenly.
7. Press "Power Button" of Ninja Foodi Digital Air Fry Oven and turn the dial to select "Air Fry" mode.
8. Press "Time Button" and again turn the dial to set the cooking time to 20 minutes.
9. Now push "Temp Button" and rotate the dial to set the temperature at 320 degrees F.
10. Press "Start/Pause" button to start.
11. When the unit beeps to show that it is preheated, open the lid.
12. Arrange the pan in air fry basket and insert in the oven.

13. When cooking time is complete, open the lid and place the pan onto a wire rack to cool for about 10 minutes before serving.

Serving Suggestions: Serve with the topping of vanilla ice cream.

Variation Tip: If You want to use frozen blueberries, then thaw them completely.

Nutritional Information per Serving:

Calories: 459 | **Fat:** 12.6g|**Sat Fat:** 7.8g|**Carbohydrates:** 84g|**Fiber:** 2.7g|**Sugar:** 53.6g|**Protein:** 5.5g

Butter Cake

Preparation Time: 15 minutes
Cooking Time: 15 minutes
Servings: 6

Ingredients:

- 3 ounces butter, softened
- ½ cup caster sugar
- 1 egg
- 1 1/3 cups plain flour, sifted
- Pinch of salt
- ½ cup milk
- 1 tablespoon icing sugar

Preparation:

1. In a bowl, add the butter and sugar and whisk until light and creamy.
2. Add the egg and whisk until smooth and fluffy.
3. Add the flour and salt and mix well alternately with the milk.
4. Grease a small Bundt cake pan.
5. Place mixture evenly into the prepared cake pan.
6. Press "Power Button" of Ninja Foodi Digital Air Fry Oven and turn the dial to select "Air Fry" mode.
7. Press "Time Button" and again turn the dial to set the cooking time to 15 minutes.
8. Now push "Temp Button" and rotate the dial to set the temperature at 350 degrees F.
9. Press "Start/Pause" button to start.
10. When the unit beeps to show that it is preheated, open the lid.
11. Arrange the pan into the air fry basket and insert in the oven.
12. When cooking time is completed, open the lid and place the cake pan onto a wire rack to cool for about 10 minutes.
13. Carefully invert the cake onto the wire rack to completely cool before slicing.
14. Dust the cake with icing sugar and cut into desired size slices.

Serving Suggestions: Serve with the sprinkling of cocoa powder.

Variation Tip: Use unsalted butter.

Nutritional Information per Serving:

Calories: 291 | **Fat:** 12.9g|**Sat Fat:** 7.8g|**Carbohydrates:** 40.3g|**Fiber:** 0.8g|**Sugar:** 19g|**Protein:** 4.6g

Raisin Bread Pudding

Preparation Time: 15 minutes
Cooking Time: 12 minutes
Servings: 3

Ingredients:

- 1 cup milk
- 1 egg
- 1 tablespoon brown sugar
- ½ teaspoon ground cinnamon
- ¼ teaspoon vanilla extract
- 2 tablespoons raisins, soaked in hot water for 15 minutes
- 2 bread slices, cut into small cubes
- 1 tablespoon chocolate chips
- 1 tablespoon sugar

Preparation:

1. In a bowl, mix together the milk, egg, brown sugar, cinnamon, and vanilla extract.
2. Stir in the raisins.
3. In a baking pan, spread the bread cubes and top evenly with the milk mixture.
4. Refrigerate for about 15-20 minutes.
5. Press "Power Button" of Ninja Foodi Digital Air Fry Oven and turn the dial to select "Air Fry" mode.
6. Press "Time Button" and again turn the dial to set the cooking time to 12 minutes.
7. Now push "Temp Button" and rotate the dial to set the temperature at 375 degrees F.
8. Press "Start/Pause" button to start.
9. When the unit beeps to show that it is preheated, open the lid.
10. Arrange the pan over the wire rack and insert in the oven.
11. When cooking time is completed, open the lid and place the baking pan aside to cool slightly.
12. Serve warm.

Serving Suggestions: Serve with the drizzling of vanilla syrup.

Variation Tip: Use ode day-old bread.

Nutritional Information per Serving:

Calories: 143 | **Fat:** 4.4g|**Sat Fat:** 2.2g|**Carbohydrates:** 21.3g|**Fiber:** 6.7g|**Sugar:** 16.4g|**Protein:** 5.5g

21 Days Meal Plan

Day 1:

Breakfast: Banana & Walnut Bread

Lunch: Quinoa Burgers

Dinner: Spicy Salmon

Day 2:

Breakfast: Savory French Toast

Lunch: Crab Cakes

Dinner: Buttermilk Whole Chicken

Day 3:

Breakfast: Sweet Potato Rosti

Lunch: Stuffed Eggplants

Dinner: Spiced Pork Shoulder

Day 4:

Breakfast: Cheddar & Cream Omelet

Lunch: Tofu with Broccoli

Dinner: Parmesan Crusted Chicken Breasts

Day 5:

Breakfast: Carrot & Raisin Bread

Lunch: Herbed Bell Peppers

Dinner: Herbed Leg of Lamb

Day 6:

Breakfast: Zucchini Fritters

Lunch: Herbed Shrimp

Dinner: Buttered Turkey Breast

Day 7:

Breakfast: Ricotta Toasts with Salmon

Lunch: Feta Turkey Burgers

Dinner: Balsamic Beef Top Roast

Day 8:

Breakfast: Pancetta & Spinach Frittata

Lunch: Pita Bread Pizza

Dinner: Lamb Chops with Carrots

Day 9:

Breakfast: Savory French Toast

Lunch: Quinoa Burgers

Dinner: Lemony Chicken Thighs

Day 10:

Breakfast: Eggs, Tofu & Mushroom Omelet

Lunch: Herbed Bell Peppers

Dinner: Citrus Pork Chops

Day 11:

Breakfast: Ham & Egg Cups

Lunch: Tofu with Broccoli

Dinner: Molasses Glazed Duck Breast

Day 12:

Breakfast: Cheddar & Cream Omelet

Lunch: Veggies Stuffed Bell Peppers

Dinner: Salmon with Prawns

Day 13:

Breakfast: Sweet Potato Rosti

Lunch: Crab Cakes

Dinner: Glazed Beef Short Ribs

Day 14:

Breakfast: Pancetta & Spinach Frittata

Lunch: Feta Turkey Burgers

Dinner: BBQ Pork Chops

Day 15:

Breakfast: Ham & Egg Cups

Lunch: Quinoa Burgers

Dinner: Cod with Sauce

Day 16:

Breakfast: Ricotta Toasts with Salmon

Lunch: Spiced Shrimp

Dinner: Herbed Lamb Loin Chops

Day 17:

Breakfast: Zucchini Fritters

Lunch: Pita Bread Pizza

Dinner: Herbed Turkey Legs

Day 18:

Breakfast: Carrot & Raisin Bread

Lunch: Herbed Shrimp

Dinner: Bacon-Wrapped Chicken Breasts

Day 19:

Breakfast: Eggs, Tofu & Mushroom Omelet

Lunch: Veggies Stuffed Bell Peppers

Dinner: Buttered Strip Steak

Day 20:

Breakfast: Savory French Toast

Lunch: Cod Burgers

Dinner: Herbed Whole Chicken

Day 21:

Breakfast: Banana & Walnut Bread

Lunch: Stuffed Eggplants

Dinner: Salmon with Broccoli

Conclusion

The Ninja Foodi Digital Air Fry Oven is one of the most promising air fryers and toaster oven you can have in your kitchen. It offers various functions like air roasting, toasting, baking, keeping your food warm, dehydrating, air frying, and air broiling. Its price is very reasonable for the function it offers.